Cult Bees
& Legends

Volume Two

Cult Bees & Legends
Volume Two

Author David Lane

Published by
Legends Publishing
22 Park Road
Hampton Hill
Middlesex
TW12 1HF

Tel (0208) 255 6560
E-mail info@legendspublishing.net
Web www.legendspublishing.net

Copyright 2005 by Legends Publishing

Photos
Every effort has been made to trace the copyright holders of the photographs in this book - some have been unreachable. We would be grateful if the photographers concerned would contact us.

Notice of Rights
All rights reserved. Unless it is part of a published review, no part of this book may be reproduced or transmitted in any form or by any means, electronically or mechanical, including photocopying, recording, or by any other information storage and retrieval system, without prior written permission from the publisher. For information on getting permission for reprints and excerpts, contact Legends Publishing.

All views expressed in this book are the personal opinions of the individuals concerned and not necessarily those of the author, the publisher or the football club. All efforts have been made to ensure the content of this book is historically accurate but if any individual named feels they have been misrepresented your right to reply will be exercised if you so wish.

Foreword & Contents

*Jo, thanks for all your love and support,
to Seb my brilliant little boy, and my Princess, Darcey.*

A little over three years ago I set off on a journey which has seen me interview some of the biggest movers and shakers to have played for Brentford in the club's post-War history – to find out what it was really like to have been a Bee's player in days gone by and to record the fortunes of our club by tapping into the memories of the men who wore the red and white stripes of Brentford out there on the pitch.

I've tried to avoid the somewhat predictable, 'Best Ever Bees' approach, although most of those who have featured in Volume One and Two would certainly fit that billing, I wanted to throw the net far wider. It was important to include players of every era, however successful, or otherwise, their time at the club was. As long as they wore the stripes with pride and there was a good story to tell, they were worthy of a phone call and an interview.

Judging by the positive response of the readers and the glowing reviews that followed the publication of Cult Bees and Legends Volume One it was clear that club die-hards found the results fascinating – so the gauntlet had been thrown down to make Volume Two even better. My aim for this follow-up was to make the book bigger, and to cover an even bigger range of eras... I think I've succeeded. Virtually every season from 1936 until the present day is represented by an interviewee featured in this book.

As well as even more iconic players I've included two important Brentford managers, who offer a slightly different perspective on events under their leadership, and as a sign of respect for everything he's done at Griffin Park over the years, Peter Gilham, a fan known to all others, shares his memories on a club he describes as "the be all and end all". I've also trawled the player's personal photo collections and scrapbooks, and along with Mark Chapman, every other possible source, to ensure as many 'new' pictures as possible.

Thank you for buying Cult Bees and Legends Volume Two to add to your collections, the next instalment is already under way.

David Lane

Thanks to: Mark Chapman, Keith Wade, Martin Holland, Greville Waterman, Paul Slatery, Rita Lane and Peter Gilham.

8-21 **Dennis Heath**

22-31 **Steve Perryman**

32-45 **Gordon Phillips**

46-59 **Pat Kruse**

60-67 **Frank Blunstone**

68-75 **Richard Cadette**

76-97 **Jackie Graham**

98-115 **Ted Gaskell**

116-129 **Jim Towers**

130-151 **Francis Joseph**

152-163 **Denny Mundee**

164-171 **Johnny Brooks**

172-181 **Peter Gilham**

Dennis Heath

All good things come to an end, or so people say. But one thing is for certain, relegation from the top flight at the end of the 1946-47 season certainly meant that the good times at Griffin Park became few and far between in the years that followed their fall from grace. Brentford fans would obviously have been disappointed to drop out of the top flight, but little did supporters know at the time, that irreparable damage had been done to their club's fortunes. Not even in their most grisly nightmares could die-hards have envisaged that at least sixty comparatively barren years were to follow.

The days of the household name signings and full international first-teamers were over, along with the 30,000 plus Griffin Park crowds every other week. As a matter of course financial straightjackets were given to incoming managers instead of a new club blazer and the ability to produce local, home-grown talent became increasingly critical to the club's survival.

It must have therefore been a considerable relief to the club's Board of Directors that Alf Bew, Brentford's Youth Manager, had built an impressive squad of rookies around that era. Not only had Alf guided his young team to the semi-final of the inaugural FA Youth Cup in 1952, but several of his side were emerging as real first team contenders. Of that team, Vernon Avis, John Pearson, and more notably, Gerry Cakebread and Dennis Heath, were fast-tracked. The latter duo becoming first team regulars for many years.

Dennis Heath was a fast, energetic winger who set up countless goals for players like Jim Towers and George Francis - to name just two. Heath was also a hugely popular squad member and knew how to find the net himself too.

Through his sons Steve and Dave, I've been fortunate enough to get to know Dennis over the past few years and a friendlier, more fun loving man, you couldn't wish to meet. Heath and sons run a successful building and decorating business in Isleworth, so if you'd like a real Brentford character to help you with some home improvements, they are listed in Yellow Pages and Thomson's Local.

Can you remember back to when you were first picked up by Brentford and talk us through your early career?

I got spotted when I was just fifteen years old playing for a team called Alexandra Villa in the Acton, Brentford and Chiswick League. Alexandra Villa was a club made up from players who lived on our estate in Chiswick. There were three big blocks of flats and everyone played football back then. I remember our clubhouse was an old scout hut that had been used to house Italian prisoners of war. Both of my brothers, John and Frank, played in that team with me and it was a very good side.

Although I was the only one to sign for a professional club I'm sure there were others that were good enough. We were playing one day when

Alf Bew, the manager of Brentford's juniors, stopped in his car as I was setting off to walk home. He asked me if I'd like to come and play for his team. Alf always had his little dog with him, it was his trademark. We trained on Tuesdays and Thursdays and turned into a very good side.

Our team had a really good FA Youth Cup run in 1952-53 when we fought our way through to the semi-finals, eventually losing out to Manchester United at Old Trafford. Their's was a superb team, they really were The Busby Babes, and we lost heavily on aggregate in the end. Eight of them were full time professionals. Unfortunately three of that United side; Duncan Edwards, David Pegg and Eddie Colman, died in the Munich air crash.

There were still a lot of big names at Brentford at the time I joined, the likes of Ron Greenwood, Jimmy Hill, Tommy Lawton, Bill Slater and Jimmy Bloomfield were all on the books. They were all very good to the youngsters and helped us whenever they could, but I have to admit I never warmed to Jimmy Hill.

I progressed at Brentford and started to train full time, but everyone had to do National Service in those days, which meant that I had to move away for two years. I was posted up to Catterick. Brentford manager Tommy Lawton wanted me closer to Brentford though, so I could get weekend passes out to play for The Bees, but the powers that be at Catterick were having none of it. There were sixteen other professionals based up there with me including Albert Quixall, who later played for Manchester United and England, plus numerous boxers and cricketers - everyone had to do National Service no matter what you did.

I was told that I was to become a PT instructor, which obviously helped to keep me fit, and I got friendly with Dougie Padgett and Gordon Barker who were really good county cricketers at the time. They invited me to join their team during the summer, but because they were so good as opening batsmen, I don't think I ever had to come to the crease once. Nobody at that level was able to bowl them out.

So was it straight out of the Army and straight in to the first team?

Yes, Brentford had me on a retainer, so I came out a pro and was drafted straight into the starting line-up. The Bees had been relegated to the Third Division South and had changed managers by the time I was demobbed, Bill Dodgin [Snr.] replacing Tommy Lawton who moved to Arsenal.

The first time I realised that I may be about to get picked for the first team was during pre-season before the start of 1954-55. Bill Dodgin arranged a 'Stripes versus Whites' practice game where the reserves took on the first team, I was invited into their dressing room for the first time and later told that I was going to make my debut against

Southampton at The Dell the following Saturday. I'll always remember the team sheet being pinned to the wall that day and seeing my name on it.

Your debut must have seemed a baptism of fire, do you remember the ten goal thriller at Southampton?
It certainly was a debut and a half, Brentford were a goal down within twenty seconds and six-one down at half time. We fought back in the second half though and got the score back to six-four. We could have scored even more too, I had a couple of shots that went inches past the post, which I thought were going in. But Bill Dodgin told me I should be happy with my performance and I kept my place in the side.

As a youngster breaking in to the team, how did you find the manager?
Bill Dodgin was a good manager, the kind that you wanted to play well for. Like his son he wasn't a disciplinarian and it was hard not to like the man. He always encouraged me. Bill was a good dancer too!
One of the Directors, Mr. Wheatley, a frail man with a lovely house, always used to throw big parties. The cha-cha dance had just come out over here and I remember all the players and the manager prancing round at Christmas after a few drinks. The training under Bill Dodgin and Tommy Eggleston wasn't great though, there was little variety, just lots and lots of running. We virtually trained ourselves in all honesty.

Who were your closest friends in the team?
I was closest to Bill Goundrey and Jim Towers in those early years, they were around the same age as me and in a similar position to myself- trying to establish themselves at the club. Jim Towers was a special footballer I thought, I vividly remember him scoring on his debut, just after mine, near the beginning of the 1954-55 season. I also got on really well with George Stobbart, a forward who came to Brentford from Millwall. George was a bloody good player. But he was a lot older than myself which meant it was difficult to get too friendly.

You had a pretty good record in front of goal and only had to wait four games before getting off the mark didn't you?
I don't really remember my first goal unfortunately, which was at home to Queen's Park Rangers in a one-all draw, but I certainly remember my second the following week away at Brighton. They had a lovely pitch down there and we beat them four-three, Jim Towers got the first, then a couple of minutes later I popped up on the left and scored too.
I scored a more important goal than that down at Brighton though, right near the end of the 1957-58 season. Brentford and Brighton were

neck and neck at the top of the division and with four games to go there was virtually nothing in it. Two of those four games were against Brighton, home and away. I scored in the one-all draw at their place in front of over 25,000, then just over a week later, we beat them one-nil at Griffin Park in front of an even bigger crowd.

It was our final game of the season and the victory meant we were top of the league and in the only promotion spot. Brighton had a game in hand though, two days later against Watford.

Jim Towers and myself decided to go out on the night of the deciding match, we didn't really drink back then, so we were in a place called the Open City in Richmond, having a minute steak and a coffee, when the score came in. Six-nil to Brighton! We had missed out on promotion.

We were so angry, the players were convinced that something dodgy had gone on because we knew Watford weren't that bad a team, in fact they'd beaten us four-one earlier in the season. For them to roll over like that seemed unbelievable. I have to admit that the talk among the team was of a fixed match, nothing could be proved, but in those days it could have been possible for a club to get away with something like that.

Do you have a favourite goal?
One of my most memorable goals was at home to Norwich in 1959. Over 21,000 were at Griffin Park for that one and I scored to put us two-one up just before half time. George McLeod out on the left went past the full-back and crossed it perfectly, I didn't have to adjust, the ball virtually hit me on the head and flew into the goal. It felt fantastic to see it crash into the net and hear the crowd roar.

The balls we had to play with were appalling though, no wonder shots went wide. Some of those great, big, heavy, lace-up things weren't even round. I remember scoring one goal where I took a free kick and the ball swerved so much in the air, not because I had deliberately curled it, but because it was almost oval. The goalie didn't stand a chance.

Season 1954-55 was a very eventful year, not only for yourself, but for the whole side. There had been a lot of changes from the previous season and under Bill Dodgin we played good, attacking football and finished mid-table. But the highlight of the campaign was the FA Cup run which saw The Bees progress to the Fourth Round and a trip to Newcastle. What do you remember about playing in front of 45,000 at St. James' Park?
Well we stayed up in Whitley Bay for the whole week leading up to the cup-tie and trained on the sands. It was freezing cold with the wind blowing in off the North Sea, but with sand and salt blasting us, training was a dead loss really. The night before the game all the older players decided to

1954-55 Dennis Heath (third from right) and the team in Whitley Bay before the Newcastle Cup tie.

sit in the hotel and play cards, so me and Jim Towers decided to sneak out, but not for a drink or anything like that. We were only young and wanted to get out for a walk and have a good look around.

The weather had turned really icy and as a precaution Newcastle had covered the pitch with tons of straw to protect the grass from the frost. The club had got loads of Scouts and Brownies to help clear the pitch before kick-off and they had piled it up near the edge of the playing area. When Newcastle scored I remember the Scouts throwing loads of straw up in the air all round the ground, but when we got one in, nothing!

We did really well up there and almost held out for a two-all draw, John Rainford and George Stobbart got our goals. In all honesty we gave the game away really. A mess up between Sonny Feehan in the Brentford goal and John Rainford let their winger, Mitchell, nip in and square it for Vic Keeble to net the winner. I can still see it in my head in slow motion, Sonny bowling the ball out to Johnny, who was out of position, and made a right mess of things. I looked on wondering what the hell the pair were up to!

Bill Dodgin often used to say that "football was a game of mistakes, if people didn't make mistakes then nobody would ever win", but it would have been great to have held out for a draw and got them back to Griffin Park.

But it took three games against Bradford City in the Third Round before Brentford finally got the chance to play Newcastle?

I played in the first two, but Bill Dodgin took me to one side and explained that he was going to drop me for the second replay, which was played at Arsenal. Bill thought he had lined up a transfer for Billy Dare, so he wanted to make room for him in the side. I wasn't happy but the switch worked out for the manager because Billy got the winning goal at Highbury and moved to West Ham for £10,000 a few days later.

Brentford had another good Cup run in 1958-59 getting to the Fourth round again. This time we got knocked out at West Brom in front of another 40,000 plus crowd.

That was another big occasion and there were lots of Bees fans up at The Hawthorns on another freezing cold afternoon. My brother had a transit van and all my family drove up in it, sat on deck chairs in the back. They were so cold when they eventually arrived that my wife said she would refuse to go back in the van. In the end I asked the manager if it was okay for her to come back to London on the team bus. Bill Dodgin eventually agreed, but the family had set off before I could tell her the good news.

We didn't play too badly at West Brom but didn't get the break we needed. I remember all my mates had gone up to watch us and they all patted me on the back when I came out after the game.

1951-52 Dennis Heath [second from left, front row] and his Brentford juniors team-mates

Dennis Heath [front centre] poses with the lads in the Braemar Road stand

The teams you were in always seemed to be challenging with the best sides in the division and always finished there or there abouts, but we always seemed to fall just short. Why was that do you think?

Our team was good enough, we had some cracking players, but we never seemed to get that extra bit of luck that you needed to finish at the top of the league. Remember only one team went up from the division, so getting promoted was more difficult than ever during that era. We went so close in 1958 and 1959, and we did well against the teams that finished above us, but we couldn't drum up those extra few points.

We even thought that not washing our shirts may be the route to success when we were challenging with Plymouth in 1958-59! We beat Argyle three-nil at home in front of 29,000 over Easter, then decided not to wash the shirts until we played them at their place three days later.

We drew at Home Park but we must have stunk by the end of the game because we'd also played Bournemouth at home in between. Three games in four days! Unfortunately we lost our way a bit after those good results and finished third.

What's the story behind the Brentford team being invited to appear in a film with Diana Dors?

The film was called 'The Great Game' and a few of the players were invited down to the studios where we had a right laugh. The make-up people wet our brows so it looked like we were sweating and smeared mud on our legs for effect. We got paid £7 each for that which was pretty good at the time. I never got to meet Diana Dors herself, she wasn't even there when I was at the studio, but I do appear in the film.

That was your only brush with Hollywood then?

For me it was, yeah, but later we did have a player in the team who was on television every Sunday evening! Bill Dodgin bought a guy from Huddersfield called Jeff Taylor, he was a clumsy lump who the rest of the lads didn't really rate. He was a better singer than a footballer for sure.

He used to perform with an outfit called 'The Adams Singers' and appeared on a show called 'Sing Something Simple' every Sunday night at 6:30pm dressed up similar to the Black and White Minstrels. He was a rugged player but a right flapper, but he scored a few I suppose. I used to really enjoy the television programme though.

What do you remember most about Griffin Park and Bees fans?

Brentford always had good support at the time, we'd get 15,000 at Griffin Park most weeks and almost double that for the bigger games. On a match day there were bikes everywhere and almost every house in the surrounding block used to rent their front gardens out and let fans leave their bikes there at 3d a time. They were piled up everywhere, twenty-plus in each garden, but it's amazing, I don't think one was ever nicked.

Because there were more Brentford fans around in those days, getting spotted out and about was always a problem, me and Jim Towers were recognised everywhere we went and even followed around sometimes. I still get stopped in the street from time to time by older Brentford fans and it's always nice to talk to them about the old days.

I also remember that we played an awful lot of midweek floodlight games at Griffin Park, against teams from all over the place. We even played a Brazilian team by the name of Botafogo at Brentford. Floodlights were fairly new and the evening games were very popular, there were some good crowds for those friendly matches and the players didn't mind playing in them as we got extra money on top of our wages.

How would you describe yourself as a player?
I was fit, I could have been better, but I suppose I wasn't really good enough. What got me through, and impressed four successive Brentford managers to keep me on, was my attitude I think. I always used to head up training, to the annoyance of some of the older players, and I was always keen which helped me.

I was quick too, until one game at Charlton when I got clattered by a player called Syd Ellis. Jack Holliday, the trainer, came on and waved some smelling salts under my nose, then tried to help me to my feet, but I knew I was in big trouble. The club doctor, Eric Radley-Smith, then came and had a look at me before I was taken to the Brentford Cottage Hospital. They discovered that I'd broken a rib, which in turn had punctured my lung.

They sealed off part of my lung instead of cutting me right open and trying to repair it all, but I almost died in that hospital one night. This big, fat nurse by the name of Blossom, I'll never forget her name, was sweeping up the ward when her broom got caught up in the tubes that were stitched in to me. She accidentally pulled them right out of my lung and I thought I was a goner. I was moved to a specialist lung ward at Harefield after that incident. The injury finished me really, I did play again, but I never got my pace or strength back and Malcolm McDonald eventually got rid of me.

I had a tooth smashed out at Griffin Park too, against Arsenal in a London Floodlight Cup match. Tommy Docherty knocked me about all night but it was their goalie, Jack Kelsey, that did the damage. I went up for a header, but instead of punching the ball clear he punched me straight in the gob.

So where did you go after The Bees?
I went into the Southern League and played for Bedford Town under Ronnie Rourke who used to play for Arsenal, then I moved to Trowbridge in Wiltshire, then Dover, before a player-manager's job at Chertsey Town.

I carried on playing until I was sixty though, for Eversheds in a local veteran's league. There was a fantastic social scene at Eversheds and football continued to be a big part of my life, training on a Wednesday, fish and chips for fifteen afterwards, then there was always a party or a disco in the club house on a Saturday night after our game.

But as far as Brentford goes, I couldn't have been at a better club, the supporters were great to me and there were lovely people who worked at the club. I'd love to be able to do it all again, I really would.

Steve Perryman

If ever there was a Brentford manager with potential it was Steve Perryman. The former Spurs icon, who amassed over a thousand appearances in the colours of the north London giants at every level from schoolboy all the way up to UEFA Cup winner, set about dragging Brentford up by the scruff of the neck and laid the foundations that would see our club rise out of the bottom two divisions for the first time in almost half a century.

Perryman was signed from Oxford United, where he'd spent a short period after leaving White Hart Lane, by Frank McLintock for his playing prowess, but it wasn't long before ex-Spurs took over from ex-Arsenal at the helm and Bees fans were treated to an exciting change in fortunes.

Steve Perryman made some inspired signings at Brentford and also used the lessons learnt from his immense playing experience to educate the players he inherited. Dean Holdsworth, Gary Blissett, Keith Jones, Richard Cadette, Neil Smillie, Alan Cockram, Simon Ratcliffe, John Buttigieg and Roger Stanislaus were all signed by Perryman, and will be remembered as some of the most exciting players to wear the red and white stripes of Brentford in the modern era. At last The Bees were making a long-overdue metamorphosis, shedding their hopeful pretenders skin and emerging as genuine promotion contenders. And who will ever forget the monumental FA Cup run which saw Brentford fight their way through to a quarter-final showdown against Liverpool at Anfield in 1989, after eliminating Manchester City and Blackburn Rovers?

The history books will always show that it was Phil Holder who finally guided Brentford out of Division Three in 1992, but nobody can fail to recognise that, apart from one or two alterations, it was fundamentally Perryman's team that won the Championship that season. As you will read in the following interview, conducted at Steve's home in Gerrard's Cross, the end of his Brentford reign, and the timing of his departure, are still a big regret to the man. Some Brentford fans still share the same feelings.

What made you come to Brentford in the first place? After playing 655 league games for Spurs surely you didn't need to carry on playing?

Well, Brentford were local, my Dad's family was from Hounslow, my Mum's family was from Gunnersbury Avenue and I used to go and watch The Bees as a youngster. The fact that they were playing at a level where I thought I could still compete was another factor, but in the back of my mind, because I'd been involved in the top flight for so long, I knew I had to drop down and broaden my knowledge of the game if I wanted to get into management.

When the chance came to manage Brentford it was perfect for me, as a footballer you spend so much time away from home that to have such a great opportunity virtually on my doorstep was fantastic. It's a recipe for domestic disaster to have a lot of travelling time on top of the twelve hours you have to put into managing a team every day.

Frank McLintock was the manager who brought you to Griffin Park, didn't he shoot himself in the foot by bringing in his successor?

To be fair Frank encouraged me to come to Brentford knowing it could be a good opportunity for me. I'd always respected Frank as a player and I often saw him at Tottenham, we always had a drink together whenever we bumped into one another. I thought he'd be a good man to learn something from as his assistant, as well as having something left to offer as a player. So all things pointed towards a good partnership.

Once you'd been given the chance to manage Brentford on a full time basis you set about transforming the side and you're remembered for bringing in some very exciting players.

I think you're right. I had to make something out of nothing, I've always liked a challenge! I think I've proved in my time in Japan, though, that I can be equally successful at developing the players I've got opposed to just using the transfer market. Today, I'd be nervous of spending the kind of money that some of the Premiership managers spend.

What were your priorities when you were given control of the team?

Well my first thoughts were that there was so much wrong with the club I must be able to make an improvement. The first thing I changed wasn't on the pitch though, it was the washing machine in the boot room. It had been leaking for ages and as normal at Brentford, nobody had ever got round to putting it right. Water was slopping about all over the place and the players' boots were getting saturated.

But not only did the boot room serve as a laundry and storage area, it was also the club's weight room, where the recuperating players were supposed to aid their rehab. Both Terry Evans and Bob Booker were coming back from cruciate knee ligament injuries and were expected to spend hours at a time in there, whenever they picked up some weights they found them dripping. Forget space-aged gymnasiums, at Griffin Park things were so basic they were untrue. I knew that I could improve the set-up. I'd have been stupid if I'd failed.

I take it you don't consider yourself as stupid then?

[Laughs] No, I enjoyed my time there on the whole and I felt there were big improvements on and off the pitch from that era.

So why did it go so wrong for you so suddenly?

Well, things started to go wrong after we lost Roger Stanislaus. Phil Holder had done a great job tracking Roger at Arsenal and he'd been on his trail for a while. Phil was even interested after being stood up three times by the player when he was supposed to be coming to meetings. Eventually Roger turned up, Phil got his man with the 'great left foot', and he went on to do a very good job.

Anyway, Stanislaus eventually got tempted to Bury and Brentford had to settle for £90,000 at a transfer tribunal, which wasn't the end of the world considering we'd picked him up for nothing.

On the way back from the tribunal, the Chairman asked me who I wanted to bring in as a replacement, so I said, I want Gary Elkins, Fulham's left-back. Lange asked me why. So I told him that as far as I was concerned Brentford's best player was Andy Sinton and whenever we played Fulham, Sinton never got a kick.

I take it Lange didn't share your high opinions of Elkins?

I'd done my homework and found out that Fulham would have let him go on a free at Christmas, before back-tracking, but all the evidence stacked up that if Brentford had gone to a tribunal themselves we were going to get him on our terms more or less.

The clubs were in the same division at the time and if the panel did demand a fee, it was hardly going to be a big one, £10,000 max. The Chairman obviously didn't want to sign Elkins and I couldn't get him to explain why. Eventually he conceded that he was worried that the tribunal would ask for more than he could afford, he said that they might demand as much as £50,000.

I was so certain that he was wrong that I promised Lange that whatever cost the tribunal set I would pay the sum personally. That's how much I wanted the player.

How could he refuse that offer?

Well, he still didn't agree to Elkins, he was worried what people would say about his manager having to cough up for a player if the story got out. I was determined to get the player, I wouldn't have risked my own money otherwise, but then things got really silly.

In one conversation with the Chairman he said that one of the reasons he didn't want me to sign Elkins was because Terry Bullivant had told Lange that he thought the Fulham player had 'shifty eyes'!

If looks were an issue it's a good job you weren't after Martin Keown!

[All laugh] Well it wasn't a laughing matter at the time, it boiled down to a question of trust. What the Chairman was inadvertently telling me was that he'd rather trust the judgement of one of his players than his manager's, not based on footballing ability, but facial expression. Terry Bullivant didn't like his eyes and he was prepared to fall out over the issue.

So what happened between then and you walking out on Brentford?
Well time was ticking along and Elkins could have been snapped up at any time by any club - so I went back in to see the Chairman. I told him that we were starting to prepare for the start of the season and it was my genuine belief that Brentford would get promoted if we signed Elkins. I told Lange that if he went anywhere else I was leaving, it was as simple as that. He looked me in the face and said, "you wouldn't do that", I just said, "watch me."

Elkins signed for Ray Harford at Wimbledon in the top flight, although I'd never considered Wimbledon a proper Premiership team. Harford was Elkins' manager at Fulham, he knew him best of all, and if he thought he was capable of doing a job against the likes of Tottenham, Liverpool and Manchester United every week, then he was more than able to do a good job at Brentford.

The tribunal fee set for a jump of two divisions, was just £20,000. So between two Third Division clubs it would have been peanuts. Obviously the wages were better at Wimbledon, but we could have signed Elkins long before Wimbledon or anyone else came in.

So you resigned?
Yep, I phoned him up and said that I was off, but I made the decision that I would go quietly and intentionally held back from making waves, which kind of backfired because there were subsequently a lot of quotes made up by the press about 'Steve Perryman being unable to motivate the players'. I successfully sued some of the newspapers over that, because my reputation was being damaged over something that simply wasn't true.

Do you think Lange's decision not to back your judgement on Elkins had anything to do with Eddie May's transfer from Hibernian, to replace Andy Sinton, not working out?
Eddie May was a good footballer, but I didn't feel he was mentally strong enough. Let's be honest, you can't be 100% successful in the transfer market all the time, if a Chairman expects that, he's living in another world.

Martin Lange was a clever man, he came up with the system for the play-offs etc., and he certainly didn't do Brentford any harm, but he didn't take the club to where it could have been, where it had the potential to go. He was one of these people who had a negativity about him, something in-built. When his head hit the pillow at night I think he had a little voice that would say to him, "somebody's nicking off me, someone's stitching me up..."

He wasn't a constricting Chairman, but I couldn't see why he didn't see the bigger picture, what was just around the corner. What could be achieved by going that extra yard.

Did we have to sell Andy Sinton?

For the player we did yes. Oxford manager, Maurice Evans, almost signed Sinton from Brentford for £125,000, Andy was interested in the move, but I persuaded him that Brentford was a bigger club and if he signed a new contract, if a genuinely better side came in for him, I'd let him know. Based on trust he signed again for Brentford, so I was duty bound to let the player know when QPR came in with £325,000.

If you look at the negative side of the coin, yes, I sold Andy Sinton to the club's biggest rivals, but on the positive, I gained the club an extra £200,000. I needed my players to trust me- but maybe the Brentford fans didn't because of that deal?

Andy Sinton was once described to me as a 'fat-arsed waster' because of his build, but we worked and worked on him and Sinton became one hell of a player. It still puzzles me how a right-footed player preferred to play on the left-wing, but it worked.

So what did you think when Phil Holder took over what was effectively your team and the club got promoted?

It's a big regret, but I thought 'fair play to Phil' to be honest. He brought in Billy Manuel from Gillingham and made some alterations, but the fact is that Brentford hadn't been out of the bottom two divisions for forty-odd years, not only did they get out, but they won the league and had a very valuable squad.

I've got great respect for Phil, but he knew that Brentford's Championship in 1992 wasn't just about that season, it was about the groundwork that had been done before it. But in saying that, look how Phil was treated! His crime was getting the team promoted out of a division the Chairman didn't deserve to be promoted out of.

Looking back at some of the signings you made at Brentford, Gary Blissett's was arguably the best. But is there any truth in the rumour that you were offered both Blissett and David Platt when you approached Crewe for the striker?

Yes, there is something in that, but we just couldn't afford both of them, although it wouldn't have cost us too much more than the £65,000 we paid for Blissett. Perhaps as little as £35,000 for David Platt. But you could have bought any of Crewe's players at the time.

Do you ever look back and regret that you weren't there to finish the job off at Griffin Park or be the one holding the trophy in the Championship photos?

I always look back to that time. Of course there were highs and lows, but Brentford were definitely on a roll and were improving all the time. I

1990: Steve Perryman glares at his assistant Phil Holder at Leyton Orient

felt I was starting to change some attitudes within the club too. I'd proved to the Chairman that I had a trustworthy opinion and good judgement, that I wasn't a 'taker'. I was prepared to put back everything that I learned from the game, I even used to get out and spend two hours watering the pitch from time to time!

Obviously the improvements weren't all about me, Keith Loring was doing a lot of good things off the pitch and Peter Gilham was wonderful behind the scenes. Brentford were emerging as a proper football club, as it always used to be when I went as a kid. My heart was set on making Brentford an impressive football club again.

There was a lot of momentum building with good press for what was being achieved on the pitch as well as the great community work off of it. We even got awarded an England schoolboy match at Griffin Park.

That was a funny story, I remember speaking to the guy from the FA about setting up the fixture - he said "do you want to host England v Sweden or England v Brazil?" Which one do you think I plumped for?

"Brazil please!" There was a crowd of over 10,000 at Griffin Park that night, 8,000 of which had never been to the stadium before. To me that was a huge success, seeing all those kids coming to Brentford for the first time was a fabulous achievement, one that should have been built upon more successfully.

Apart from the unfortunate final chapter, how do you look back at your time at Griffin Park over all?

In some respects Brentford was my best job, although I saved Watford from going down from an unbelievably bad position. But in terms of building up a club, it was as good a job as I've done so far. But there was a lot of scope to do that, there was a lot of weakness to strengthen, it would have been difficult not to have improved Brentford.

Under your leadership the team got through to the Quarter Finals of the FA Cup, an amazing achievement. Was there any stage during that Cup run that you thought we could actually get to Wembley or even win it?

No. I'm always realistic, which can be seen as a weakness I guess, but also a strength. In the end the Cup run was all about how much we could earn along the way. We had some great results and a fantastic reception from the Liverpool crowd at the end, which I thought was their way of congratulating us on the way we went there and tried to play. You've got to be stupid to go there and play them at 'football', but I refused to turn my back on my principles and I told the players to go out there and 'play'. We could have been a goal up, which could have meant we'd have lost six-one, but to me the result at Blackburn was the most wonderful day. In term of result, performance, tactics, Blissett's two goals - everything!

The game against Manchester City was more a typical Cup result, big team versus little team, away from home in a small ground, in those kind of situations the underdogs can win. But Blackburn was far more deserved and far more special.

Another memorable game I recall from your time as manager was away at Ashton Gate on New Year's Day 1988. Brentford won three-two after being three up in a very hostile atmosphere. To rub salt into the City fans' wounds you sent the players out for a warm-down as the supporters were still leaving the ground, which made for a treacherous walk back to our car... In fact, I was chased all the way. What made you do that?

[Laughs] They would have probably chased you anyway. I got a lot of letters about that, yeah! I remember Brentford being three up after about twenty minutes against Joe Jordan's side, so he decided to bring himself on at half time. It then became three-one, then three-two... So I decided I'd better bring myself on too.

We had Wayne Turner and Graham Rix in the side at the time and I told them to keep hold of the ball, which is what we did. It was such an un-Third Division game, it was incredible, real quality from both sides and we hung on for the points.

Gordon Phillips punches clear of Notts County's Charlie Crickmore at Griffin Park in 1971

Gordon Phillips

Gordon Phillips' name conjures up a very late 60s, early 70's vision... Lots of hair and lots of Fourth Division Football at Griffin Park. Fans had to endure some very average players during that era, but it would be wrong to tar everyone with the same brush. It was highlighted in the first volume of Cult Bees & Legends that some of the club's most influential players established their reputations during The Bee's darkest days.

As we've discovered, Brentford managers during that period had to perform miracles with wafer thin squads, so if a player wasn't pulling his weight or contributing something significant to the side, they were got rid of.

It is therefore a testament to Gordon Phillips' ability that he served under five consecutive managers at Brentford; making his debut for Malcolm McDonald in 1963, then subsequently guarding the net for Tommy Cavanagh, Billy Gray, Jimmy Sirrel and then Frank Blunstone.

After a gap of more than twenty years Gordon made a surprise return to Griffin Park in the early-90s, helping manager Phil Holder on the training ground and coaching the club's goalkeepers; Graham Benstead and Ashley Bayes.

Gordon is a modest, unassuming man who gave a fascinating and open appraisal of his time at the club and life in general for a goalkeeper almost forty years ago.

So how does the Gordon Phillips football story begin?
I was a local boy who started off with Hayes, I only played a couple of first team games, but I played at every other level for the club. In fact Dave Bassett was a team mate of mine while I was there. I wasn't exactly the tallest of goalies, so becoming a professional was always going to be difficult. I've still got lots of rejection letters from the likes of West Brom, Portsmouth, Leicester and West Ham telling me that because of my height, 5ft 10in, they weren't prepared to take me on despite a good trial or an impressive game while a scout had been watching. So when Brentford came in for me I was delighted. I'd been at Crystal Palace a little while, but I was very young and the travelling from West London was too much, so to come to Griffin Park was perfect for me.

What was life like for a young 'keeper at Brentford in the early 1960s?
An education, it really was! Tommy Cavanagh, the assistant to manager Malcolm McDonald, was a great inspiration to me as our trainer and I've still got a great deal of admiration for the man. I am grateful for the way he helped me, he was a good man. He'd tear you to pieces if you did something wrong, and he would be amongst the crowd to sort them out if he felt they were out of order or giving a player grief undeservedly, he used to say it was "his right", I'll always remember him saying that.

But once you arrive at a professional club everything changes as a player, your outlook becomes different and you have to become far more focused on the game. Football becomes more serious, mortgage payments are dependent on your form or health and you have to stay at the top of your game otherwise you know you're out.

You also had the upkeep of a rather large tash to worry about!
[Laughs] Yes, everyone still goes on about that. I'm friendly with lots of Brentford fans that work with me at British Airways who love reminding me about my moustache days, even after almost thirty years in the job! There were a lot of far hairier players than me in that early-seventies team.

It appears you had a very busy first few weeks at Brentford, the record books show that you conceded thirteen goals in your first two reserve and junior games, then two more on your first team debut to Margate in the FA Cup at Griffin Park.
Yes I let in a howler at home against Margate. We were winning two-one inside the last ten minutes when I fumbled a header, the ball squirming through my hands and into the net. I was gutted as I thought I'd played well until then, but a lack of concentration at the split second when I was thinking about what to do with the ball after I'd gathered it meant that we had to play a replay down at their place. Fred Rycraft was back in goal for the second game and Brentford won two-nil. So it was back to being the understudy for me, but I was only young - raw goalies have to learn the hard way at times.

Chic Brodie emerged as the experienced, first choice goalie for a while, what was he like as a mentor?
Charlie was a lovely man, a super fella, and I got on really well with him. I got to know his family well and to this day the first Christmas card that comes through our letter box every year is from his wife Pam, even though Charlie is no longer with us.

Charlie helped me a lot at Brentford in those early years, and later on encouraged me when I was keeping him out of the team and he thought he should be playing. He never once took it out on me. There was never any animosity between us, he'd always come into the dressing room and see me before a game and give me a pep talk, geeing me up by drumming in positive, simple instructions for the game ahead.

But what I didn't know was that he'd be straight back outside the dressing room having a go at the manager for not being picked. No player likes being left out of the side. But whether it was Charlie or myself in goal, we always remained friends.

For want of a better word, Chic's career was 'dogged' by injuries and that infamous canine incident at Colchester. It doesn't seem fair that people talk less about his goalkeeping ability than his mishaps does it?

Not at all, Charlie was a vastly experienced 'keeper and a very good one too. Other professional footballers don't enjoy the fact that a dog on the pitch at Layer Road ended his career, and I can remember Ian St. John saying just that on his TV show some years back. It was so out of order that the animal wasn't controlled sooner, it had been around the pitch for a little while before the incident happened.

People say that the dog bit Chic, but that's not what happened, as he bent down to collect the ball the dog smashed into his knee and damaged the ligaments. Today the damage could have been repaired I expect, but in those days knee operations weren't as advanced. It annoys me when I see it replayed and people joking about it to be honest.

Did you find it frustrating waiting in the wings relying on Brodie to get injured so you could get your chance to play?

I suppose so, because like all players, you want to play, but you just have to wait for your chance and do well when it comes along. But I still enjoyed myself and loved the training. There wasn't specialised 'keepers' training like they have today and a lot of the time I played out on the pitch with the other players. I think I learned a lot more about positional play and my sense of being able to judge what to predict from outfield players developed because of that.

My understanding of the game certainly improved by being an understudy. But I did have long spells in the side when I only missed one or two games out of the whole season and over the course of other seasons Charlie and I were almost neck and neck in the games we played in.

What was Chic like as a man?

He was a very proud person, he had a bit of a temper on him too, but as I've said, he gave me every encouragement and he helped me immensely. I'll never forget going to visit Charlie when he was really ill and seeing him for the last time. I'd gone with Peter Gelson and it was terrible seeing him in such a weak, frail condition. Both Peter and myself were crying as we drove away from his house that day knowing we wouldn't see him again.

Due to the financial constraints Brentford had to operate within around 1967, the squad was whittled down to the bare bones. For the start of the 1967-68 season, the club only had fifteen players on its books... At one stage we had so few fit players that you were named as an outfield substitute. That must have made for a very closely-knit team spirit?

Gordon Phillips shows off his prize winning seventies-style tash and side-burns

Absolutely, when I joined there were about thirty-five pros at the club, then because things got so tight, big changes were made. I remember we became a very fit team, but the training was never toned down to avoid injuries. When players are fitter they recover from knocks quicker in any case, your body seems to repair itself faster when you're in good condition.

In those days it was normal for a player to continue turning out if they had a knock, today nobody seems to play unless they are 110% fit, which has been proven to be far more sensible. There was always a great spirit at the club and six or seven of that team are still in close contact today, in fact at the Griffin Park Centenary Day there were probably more players from my era there than from any other time. Alan Hawley was my best man, I was his, and Peter Gelson, who now lives in Qatar, and myself have been great pals for over forty years now. So a lot of lasting friendships were built during those years and a lot of the wives are still in regular contact with each other too.

You got your longest spell in the side while Jimmy Sirrel was the manager, what did you think of him?

Jimmy Sirrel was a one off, a cracker jack. I'll always remember his team talks, they were hilarious, but we couldn't laugh. He used to give all the players analogies, he used to tell Peter Gelson to go out on the pitch and be 'The Giant', Gordon Neilson, who arrived for £10,000 from Arsenal, was 'The Gazelle'… His talks were crazy. I also vividly remember walking out onto the pitch at Griffin Park one weekday afternoon and hearing Jimmy's distinctive whistle echoing around the ground.

When I spotted him he was walking precariously along the guttering at the very front of the big Royal Oak stand knocking lost balls back down. Balanced about a hundred feet up, it was so dangerous, if he had fallen he wouldn't have stood a chance. There was nothing to stop him falling either and there was only one massive ladder at the far end of the roof to get up and down. He certainly didn't have a fear of heights!

He also once spent several weeks helping a pigeon recover from a broken wing that he found, feeding it back to health. Then about a week after releasing it back into the wild he shot it with an air pistol because the bird was eating the grass seed from one of the penalty areas!

The players spent more time at Griffin Park than their modern day counterparts so you must have known Brentford pretty intimately. What do you remember of the ground and the surrounding area?

I always think of Griffin Park as a lovely, compact ground. There always seemed to be a cracking atmosphere and more often than not there would be a good crowd. Even when things were going badly eight thousand fans still turned up, and when things were better, double that. A lot of our training was done in and around the ground and I remember every Friday morning we used to play five-a-side on what is now the Braemar Road forecourt. We used to call that area 'Little Hampden'.

I always remember walking to the ground after getting off the bus and seeing gardens full of bikes and we used to go and get our lunch in the Bricklayer's Arms pub after training. Win or lose we'd always go out for the night locally after a game too. I used to love playing at Griffin Park.

What grounds didn't you like playing at?

I used to hate going to Southend, I don't know why, but we never seemed to do well there and I've got some bad memories about that place. Brighton was another ground I hated playing at. None of the grounds were exactly glamorous though, we had to go to places like Bradford Park Avenue, Workington and Barrow, towns where you never saw the sky. Hartlepool was pretty grim too. At Barrow you had to walk through a hole in a wall to get to the bath after a game, it was pretty basic up there.

What was the funniest thing that happened to you in a match?

The goal that never was against Southend! Pat Terry was the hardest header of the ball I've ever seen and when he first arrived I remember being gob-smacked when he used to practice headers using the back of his head. He had this amazing skill of watching a cross come over, jumping to head the ball, then at the last split-second, move his head the other way and glance it in the opposite corner to where you thought he was going to put it. At first I thought it was a fluke, but he did it over and over again.

One day he was showing off and I bet him he couldn't do it again, so John Docherty put over a lovely cross and he jumped and did his trick, I heard the ball hit the net but we couldn't find the ball in the back of it. We searched for the ball for ages before realising that the net wasn't secured properly at the side, so when the ball hit it in a certain place, it rolled down, went through a hole, then rolled off the side of the pitch. We didn't think anything more of it until the following Saturday.

Then, in a match against Southend, the same thing happened. Southend had a corner, the ball came over and Gary Moore beat a defender to the ball and headed past me. Goal! But the ball had hit the exact same spot and appeared to go out for a goal-kick. I suspected what had happened because I'd heard the net go, but I just collected the ball and took the goal kick. A few of the opposition players were left very bewildered though.

How did you rate yourself as a 'keeper?

Well, it's been said by a lot of people throughout my career, "if I were three or four inches taller then I would probably have done better in the game", but I tried to make do with what I had. I didn't mind diving around down at people's feet and getting hurt trying to get the ball, and I was lucky that I had Peter Gelson in my defence because what I lacked in aerial strength he made up for.

He was my star really, he would take care of everything around me and on his day he was as good as anyone in the game I thought. Peter was at his best when he was ruthless with forwards. We had a great understanding, and more often than not, the combination worked.

But I don't think I was anything special. Because of my height it was always going to be a battle for me, but I knew that from an early age. I trained hard and loved it, in fact I still do, but there was nothing I could do about getting taller.

As a goalkeeper did you separate yourself from the rest of the side at times? Did you ever think that as long as you kept a clean sheet or didn't make a mistake it was up to the outfield players to do their bit and win games?

Yes I probably did at times, you feel under the spotlight when you're in goal and your form certainly has an effect on the other players. If you're confident and command your area, shouting out orders to the defenders, whilst not making any mistakes yourself, you can play a big part in the outcome of some games.

Sometimes if Roger Cross popped up and scored at the other end late on I felt I'd played a part in that by making sure all was well in my area and allowing the other players to feel more confident and go on and win the game. I tried to keep things simple and not get myself into trouble by coming for balls I shouldn't be going for.

You see some goalies tearing around their area trying to help chase the game or going up into the other area in the dying minutes to try and score, [laughs] I never did that!

You also enjoyed the luxury of being able to pick up back-passes and run around your area with the ball in your arms didn't you?

They've messed around with the rules too much from a 'keeper's perspective. Coming out and having to kick the ball from a back pass is okay when the pitch is perfect, but at a lower level and for children playing for the school etc., where the pitches can be uneven, it's a nightmare.

I wouldn't like to have had to cope with that. I know the powers that be want to encourage more goals, but I feel the game has suffered. They may as well go the whole way and make the goals twenty feet taller and insist on midget goalies. [Laughs] I would probably get signed up again for Brentford if that were the case.

What Gordon Phillips lacked in height, Peter Gelson made up for in aerial strength...

Brentford had a stinker of a season in 1965-66 and were relegated to the basement, was it a slight relief that Chic was in goal most of the time that campaign when the goals were raining in left, right and centre?

No, it really doesn't work like that, they were my team mates and you want to be out there with them trying to turn things round.

I was in goal for a few heavy defeats that year too, four-two against Hull and five-nil at Exeter, but if I remember rightly some of my better games came when the team was playing badly.

You find that in general some of the better 'keepers emerge from struggling sides as they get a lot more action and learn faster because they are under pressure more frequently. If you've got a shot or cross to deal with every couple of minutes in a match situation, it's the best form of practice you can get. But to answer your question again, no, I would have preferred to have played, even in that relegation fight.

Do you remember much about the 1967 take-over bid by QPR?

From a player's point of view it wasn't a very nice time at all. It was awful because we just didn't know what was going to happen. Most of the lads had families and mortgages so it was unsettling, if we got the elbow then there was a lot at risk. Ron Blindell really bailed the club out and without him I don't think there would have been a Brentford Football Club to support today.

There weren't lots of get-togethers among the players to talk about what was going on as far as I recall, but we talked about the issues a lot travelling to away games and in the New Inn or Bricklayer's after training. I guess the feeling was that everything was out of our hands really.

Arguably the biggest Brentford game you were in goal for was the FA Cup Third Round tie at Roker Park in 1967. Almost 37,000 fans saw The Bees lose five-two, do you remember the match?

Yes, we may have lost but I don't think we let ourselves down, we even went two-one up after being a goal behind early on, John Docherty got them both that day.

Sunderland were a good top flight side at the time and had some good players. Jim Baxter turned the game for them unfortunately, he was that bit better and was able to find the room to start spraying balls around.

He scored a penalty and was involved in the other goals, but it was a very good experience for all of us. I was sure I was going to save that spot-kick, I'd pumped myself up and was convinced I'd make a block, but as the whistle went he rolled it the opposite way as I dived to my right.

As a Division Four player in the mid-to-late Sixties, did you feel more equal to the footballers plying their trade in Division One, The

Premiership equivalent of the time. Was there more camaraderie amongst the leagues then?

I think we did feel more of a bond between those at the top and ourselves, yes. Things seemed friendlier and clubs would help each other out more. There were obviously still super-star players on big money, well big money compared to us, but things hadn't gone mad at that stage.

There were little things that used to happen then that wouldn't happen today probably. I remember we had a game called off somewhere up north one night and Coventry City sorted us all out tickets for their game against Stoke so we could stop off on the way home. I couldn't take my eyes off Gordon Banks that night.

What was your injury record like at Brentford?

Not bad really, I used to break fingers now and again and I've broken my nose a few times but that was par for the course for a goalkeeper back then. We weren't too protected by the rules or the referees, plus the footballs were a damn sight heavier than they are today.

In my early days at the club I remember that the players used to pick up lots of cuts and scratches, some of which used to get infected by the manure and fertilisers that was used on pitches. Then we would have preventative injections. These infections were a serious issue, Derek Dooley, who played for Sheffield Wednesday had a leg amputated after a break turned really bad, so for a couple of years at least, all the players were driven down to Brighton by coach on a Wednesday morning so we could soak in the brine at the Prince Regent Baths down there.

Every week we used to travel down and soak in the salt waters. It was great, all the players would sit neck-high in warm water around the edge of a big pool and have a right laugh telling stories and swapping tales.

But I did pick up one awkward injury at a Brentford open day at Feltham Arena one pre-season, I made a penalty save from one of the children that came along on a rock-hard surface and landed awkwardly on my hip. I must have bruised the bone or something because it really affected my mobility during pre-season games and helped lose my place in the side.

I just couldn't shake it off. I remember playing in a friendly down on the South coast shortly afterwards and I wasn't able to get down to my left to make saves. I really should've stopped playing and got it treated properly, instead of battling on and pretending everything was alright because it did me no favours in the long run.

To make matters worse an incident happened outside Griffin Park where one of the players took a swing at another. Frank Blunstone was the manager at the time and thought I'd started it out of frustration, which wasn't the case at all, and things got a bit silly after that.

So was that incident the beginning of the end for you at Brentford?
Perhaps, but not really because of that incident. I thought Frank wanted to replace me and I'd even spoken to him about it, asking him to give me as much notice as he could so I could sort myself out with another club. So I was disappointed that I found out third hand after my father-in-law was told by somebody he knew at the ground. It was a shame to leave Brentford, it's a nice club.

There was never really any bad blood between Frank and myself though, even though it upset me, I was one of the first to send him a card after he had a bad car crash while he was at Manchester United. I saw him down at Staines Town a few years back and we had a really good chat and a drink talking about the old times.

So you followed the already well-worn path and joined the long list of ex-Bees to move from Brentford to Hillingdon Borough?
Yes a lot of players made the move up the road after Brentford, well the local lads in any case. When I arrived at Hillingdon Tommy Higginson and Eddie Reeve were already there, then a little bit later, Peter Gelson and Alan Hawley joined along with Alan Nelmes and Paul Bence after them. It really was a home from home. Hillingdon was another nice friendly club, although it could get a bit naughty down there depending on what kind of crowd came in. But it was a nice ground to play at.

I had about seven years there, you don't stay somewhere that long if you don't enjoy it. A lot of the lads will tell you that they were better off at Hillingdon too, combining a 'proper' job wage with their Hillingdon appearance money, so it wasn't too hard a blow when I left Brentford, although it was difficult to accept that your professional career was over.

I did have the chance of playing in South Africa but the agent who approached me said that if I agreed to join the club in Pretoria I had to be packed and on the plane with my family within twenty-four hours, which was absolutely impossible!

You had a brief return to Brentford in the early nineties though?
Yes, Phil Holder sorted me out some coaching work with the goalies at Brentford while he was manager, it was great to come back and be involved in some way again.

I used to train Graham Benstead and Ashley Bayes and I thought Phil was a bit hard done by to get sacked after taking the club up. He was a great coach I thought and was so enthusiastic with the kids. It was a shame his management career ended like it did.

Things changed under David Webb, he wasn't friendly to the kids at all and I didn't enjoy working with him.

Did you enjoy the Centenary bash at Griffin Park and the player's reunion afterwards?

It was a great day, it really was. It was lovely seeing so many faces again, fans and players alike. I was speaking to Peter Gilham and he was saying that the club will try and get groups of players from different eras to come back to Griffin Park more regularly. I'd love to do that from time to time and I know some of my old team-mates would too.

Pat Kruse

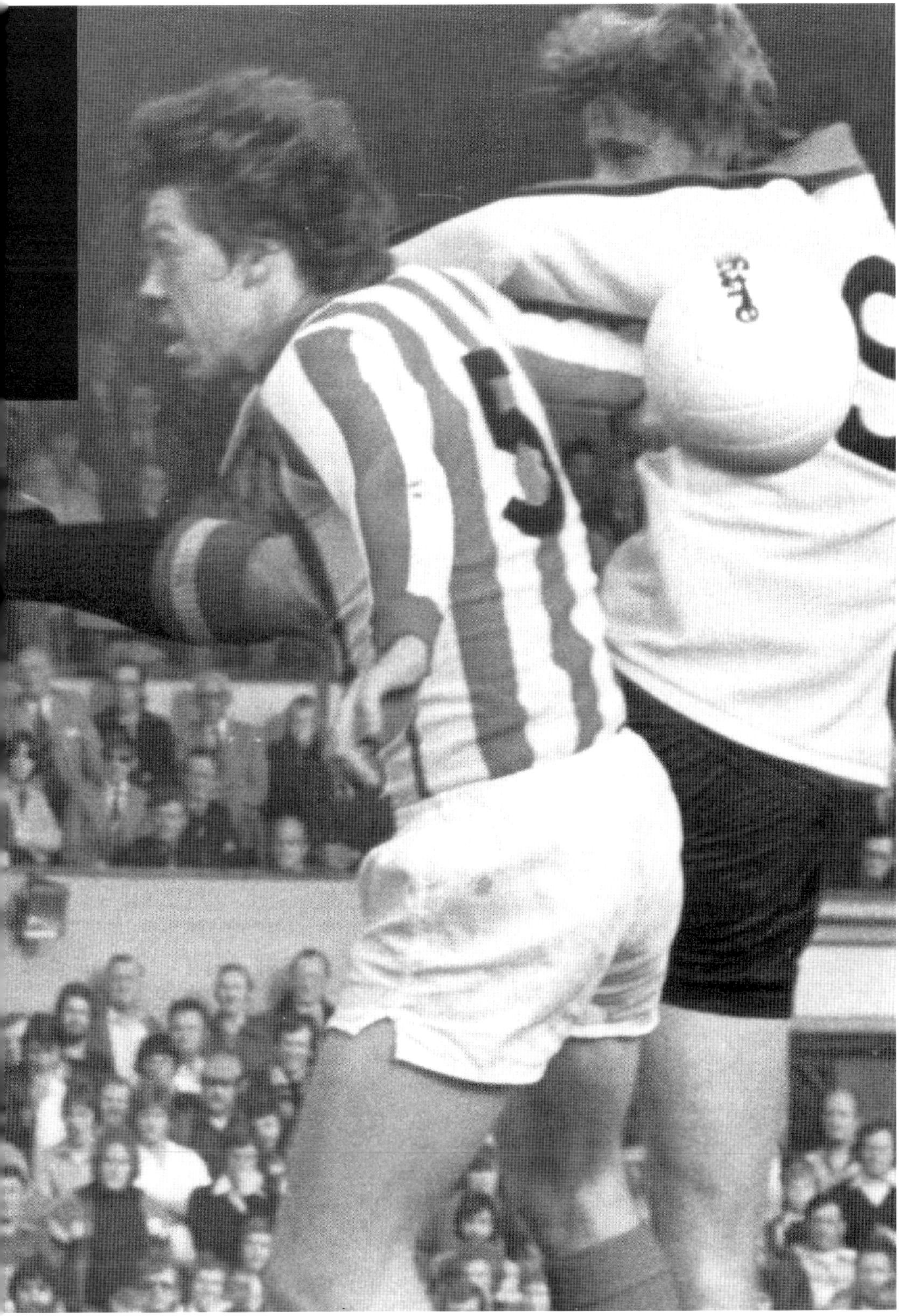

Over the past fifteen years or so I've been lucky enough to have interviewed dozens of Brentford players, but it is no exaggeration when I say none has been as frank as Pat Kruse. The former Brentford centre-back certainly pulls no punches and tells things just as he saw them, which I think makes for superb reading.

Pat arrived at Griffin Park from Torquay United just in time to cement his place in Brentford folklore, every member of Bill Dodgin's 1977-78 promotion team has a special place in the hearts of supporters who are old enough to have shared in that experience. In fact, I'd go as far as to say that 'The Class of '78' is remembered more fondly than Phil Holder's 1992 Championship winning team... And that is saying something.

There remains a lot of misty-eyed romanticism about Kruse's era, but after listening to Pat talk with so much fondness and witnessing him smile and laugh almost non-stop when reliving his time at out football club, I can understand why. Bill Dodgin made Brentford such a happy place for the players, and in turn, their enthusiasm and sense of adventure on the pitch rubbed off on the fans.

Is it any wonder, therefore, that thirty years down the line the name of Kruse and his team-mates are still talked about in pubs all over Brentford on match-days? It was a real honour to meet Pat Kruse again and a real pleasure to share his fantastic reminiscings.

Tell us about your early career, before you came to Griffin Park.
I played for my local village side Arlesey who I thought played at a very high standard and must have been spotted by a scout because when I was just about to leave school I was offered the chance to join West Ham or Leicester City. I remember wondering why I'd been the one picked out of that side to become a pro as I thought there were better players in the side than myself, but the clubs had obviously seen something that impressed them.

Looking back, going to West Ham would have been the ideal move, because if I didn't make it at Upton Park there was always a good chance another of the London sides would take me on, but I was a Leicester fan and I chose to go to Filbert Street. Frank O'Farrell was the manager at Leicester and he made the effort to travel to my village and tell me all about the club and it made all the difference, West Ham just didn't seem as keen to sign me. So I worked my way through the ranks at Leicester over the next couple of years and eventually made my debut near the end of the 1973-74 season at White Hart Lane.

It was the Martin Chivers era at Spurs, Jennings in goal and Steve Perryman of course. I then played against Norwich in the final home game and started to think I would become the regular centre-half for the following season. Unfortunately that chance went to somebody else after the summer break.

It was decided that I would go out on loan to Mansfield, which did take the wind out of my sails a bit, although The Stags had a good season and were promoted while I was there so I enjoyed it. But as a young player, when you're told you're going out on loan, it's almost like being rejected. At that age you feel the club don't want you as opposed to being farmed out to get first team experience which will allow you to return to the club a far better player.

No amount of reserve league or Combination league football at Leicester could prepare me for life in Division Four with Mansfield though, the competition was on a different level completely, and it was a real eye-opener. But I did go back to Leicester and did get back in the first team after my season at Field Mill. But after a little while the same thing happened again, Torquay manager Malcolm Musgrove, who'd worked with me at Leicester, came and asked for me to go down there and help them out as they were struggling. So I went, played well and decided to sign permanently at the end of the season. I realised things weren't going to go as planned at Leicester and decided to drop down the leagues and hoped to get spotted by a bigger club.

Whilst we're on the subject of Torquay United, I have to ask you about your World Record. What does it feel like to have scored the fastest own goal in history?
[Laughs] I'm quite proud of the fact really and I'm a bit upset that the feat hasn't been printed in recent editions, so perhaps you could start some kind of campaign to get it reinstated! I'll go through the story quickly [laughs], well, there's no other way to tell it is there?

The game against Cambridge was played in really icy conditions, just about playable in those days I'd say. Cambridge kicked off and pumped the ball forwards, being centre-half I knew I had to deal with the clearance, so I watched the ball as it came towards me just inside the area. The goalie was on my left-hand side, and I could see their forwards running, homing in. The instinctive thing to have done was to head it back as hard as I could towards the half-way line, but I decided to glance the ball back to my goalie so he could gather it, then clear to the forwards. This is where it gets a bit surreal.

Our goalie had a speech impediment, a stutter-cum-lock-jaw problem, so he came to call for the ball but no sound came out. He realised in a split second that I hadn't heard him so he tried to get back into the centre of his goal-mouth, but he slipped over on the icy grass meaning my perfectly cushioned header to him bounced twice and bobbled into the back of the net. I remember seeing the manager going mad over on the touchline, and the goal was mentioned on the Nine o'clock News and in the national newspapers. In fact the match ended two-all with Torquay scoring all four goals. We scored another own goal later in the game so the match was a real comedy of errors.

The incident obviously didn't put Brentford off buying you, how did your move to Griffin Park come about?
Again, it was through contacts made at Leicester. Bill Dodgin had worked as a coach there with me, so he must have rated me at some stage and after he'd been at Griffin Park for about six months or so he got in touch with Torquay. Brentford paid £12,500 for me and I got five per cent of the transfer fee, but there were no agents back then so I had to negotiate my own contract with the manager, which for a young lad like myself was pretty daunting.

Ironically the last game you played for Torquay was against Brentford in March 1977, Gordon Sweetzer scored a hat-trick against you and The Bees ran out three-two winners. Did you know you were moving to Griffin Park and give Sweetzer an easy time of it?
[Laughs] No I didn't, although he did give me some grief about it after I'd signed, but I honestly didn't know I was coming to Brentford at that stage. It was a bit of a relief to be moving, I realised that hardly any scouts bothered driving down to Torquay because it was such a long way, so it wasn't the best of clubs I could have moved to in Division Four to get noticed.

What did you think of Brentford when you arrived?
It was a lovely, friendly club and it was a happy place to be. The move also enabled me to move back to my home village and commute to and from Brentford to train, which was another big bonus. I jumped at the chance to join Brentford because I knew Bill Dodgin pretty well already, he used to stay in the same digs as me in Leicester and we often went out for a curry in the town in the evenings and talked about football.

Nobody I've ever spoken to who played under Dodgin has had one bad word to say about the man.
I'm from the same brigade too, Bill was a lovely man, too nice perhaps at times. Maybe it's not surprising that Bill was so liked, he surrounded himself with decent, honest players, the sort who wanted to go out and play well for him, not because he'd screamed and shouted at them before a game, but because they simply didn't want to let the man down. More often than not the players at Brentford during that era gave all they could on the pitch, it didn't work all the time, but the way we played and the effort that was put in was down to Bill.

So you never had a cross word with the manager?
No, not at all. In fact I think I only ever had one fall-out with a manager in my whole career and that was right at the end when I was playing

for Barnet. I thought Barry Fry was a complete idiot, a lot of players will agree with that, I have no idea how he has been able to bluff his way in the game for so long.

You joined a pretty formidable team by Fourth Division standards.
Yes it was a very good squad, full of seasoned players who knew their trade. There were very few youngsters in that side, apart from Danis Salman. We had John Fraser at right-back, Mickey Allen at left-back, Jackie Graham in midfield, all committed, experienced players who had played a lot at that level.

It was a very attack-minded team too, and one look at the goal-scoring stats backs that up doesn't it?
We were never directly told to go all out and attack, but it was almost that approach to be honest. Bill and the players knew that if the opposition scored a goal, we would probably score two. Bill always sent us out with confidence and I'd describe him as a football purist. He was always honest if we'd been outplayed by another team and wouldn't look for scapegoats.

We won four-nil at home on my debut and the goals kept going in at both ends for the rest of the season, in fact, Brentford failed to score in only six games during the promotion season. Bill spent time trying to tighten things up at the back, it wasn't as if he wasn't concerned because Sweetzer, Phillips and McCulloch were banging them in at the other end at an impressive rate. That's why Barry Tucker, Jim McNichol and myself were brought in.

Fred Callaghan arrived as Bill's coach about the same time as I signed and I think the two of them made the ideal 'good cop, bad cop' partnership, Fred was a good foil for Bill Dodgin and used to get us more organised in the training sessions. As far as I was concerned they provided the perfect combination of dedication and free flowing football.

Steve Phillips and Andy McCulloch were awesome weren't they?
They were good together on the pitch yes, their goal-scoring record was very impressive, helped of course by the style we played and the amount of chances that came their way. Steve did well by playing with Andy, but I thought Steve lacked something, I think he could have worked harder and scored even more.

That may seem a strange thing to say in light of the fact that he won the 1977-78 Adidas Golden Boot award, finishing as the top scorer in the whole Football League, but he only did what he had to in my view. He would never push himself and did the bare minimum required. Andy was a quite aloof individual, he seemed to think he was better than everyone

Pat Kruse and John Fraser race each other during training at the London Transport grounds

else was, which maybe he was, but a few of the lads felt he looked down his nose at us at times. He was a big, brave player though and it was good to have him in your side.

The supporters responded to Dodgin's style of play and saw the potential of your team didn't they? The attendance figures jumped massively.

I think the supporters seemed to appreciate that the players were giving it their all and when you see a packed ground, that in turn boosts the players, so it was a good combination. During that era fans could turn up at Griffin Park confident that they would probably see a home win. With Jackie Graham as captain Brentford were always going to give it everything, he was a whole-hearted player, a general, and the players responded to him.

I'll never forget playing Watford a couple of matches after I'd arrived, what a complete shock, I had no idea that the game meant so much. Jackie's blood was boiling before the game and he was barking out for us all to get stuck in, "kill the bastards", I heard him shout as the game kicked off. I thought that there'd be a blood bath as it became more and more physical with big tackles flying in. We won three-nil with all the goals coming in the opening fifteen minutes, which demonstrated how the team battled for each other and how pumped up Jackie had got the team before the start. I couldn't say one word against Jackie Graham, he epitomised everything that was good about football at the time.

You mention that win against Watford, but they were the club who eventually went on to grace the top level. Do you think Graham Taylor's approach to management would have been better at Griffin Park than Bill Dodgin's?

The two men approached the game very differently I agree, but Taylor was a lot younger and he had different ideas, Bill's experience and knowledge of the game was far greater in my view. I know a number of players who played under Graham Taylor and I am glad I wasn't one of them.

I don't know what it was but I never liked the way he had his teams play football, he had some very good players, better than ours probably, but they were playing a variation of the long-ball game, while we played a lot more football on the deck. Admittedly it brought his teams success but as a manager I think he got found out eventually because he couldn't play any other way and that style wasn't attractive.

Your centre-back partners were Paul Shrubb or Nigel Smith when you first arrived, what did you think of them as a newcomer?

Paul was another dedicated player, he was very good at what he did, he was quick and would run all day. Maybe he wasn't the most talented player in the world, but I'm being honest and I'd say that about myself too.

Nigel Smith was the reverse, skilful on the ball but a very lazy player. Sometimes his passing was amazing and he would hit a great ball, he had it in him to become a top player I thought, but he just didn't want it enough. Danis Salman played along-side me too in those early games, he was really quick and very confident, which maybe made up for what he lacked in other parts of his game at the time as I thought his passing let him down, but he matured into a very rounded defender.

What was the players' social scene like back then?
It was great, there was always something going on and I really did go out and enjoy myself. There was a close group of us that did most things together, and another that didn't come out with us very often. Players like Andy McCulloch and one or two others were on the outside slightly, but whether it was a local pub or a club up in London, the majority would be there together after a game.

Dan Tana was a great man to have as Chairman for the players' social lives, he was very well connected and he'd invite us up to The Gold Club where we'd mix in the VIP area with some of the big celebrities of the time. One night Elton John and Rick Wakeman were on the piano playing 'My Old Man's A Dustman' and 'Happy Birthday'. It was unbelievable.

We had the Player of the Year party at Hugh Hefner's Playboy Club one year too. The club's manager, who was a Brentford fan, invited us along and arranged a private bar and free drink all night for us and we were all given gold membership cards which entitled us to get in whenever we wanted. I couldn't believe it to be honest. We were nobodies really, but so often we were made to feel like A-list celebrities.

So there wasn't exactly an enforced regime of teetotalism and abstinence from the management?
Well there was a set of rules that we were asked to abide by but I can't remember many of the players sticking to them. On away trips we all used to eat together at seven o'clock, but afterwards Bill would let us do our own thing really. A couple of the players, Doug Allder and Paul Shrubb for example, would go off to bed for an early night or watch a film on television, but a core of maybe eight or nine of us would go out for a couple of pints.

We always wanted to play well the next day, so by and large it was just a quick walk around the town, not to get smashed, but to socialise and have fun together. Now I'm not saying that was always the case, at places like Blackpool and Southport the temptations were higher and I once bumped into Eddie Lyons at seven in the morning in the hotel lobby on my way back in from the night before, he thought I'd popped out to get a newspaper! It has to be said that there was the odd time when it would kick off in a

Rick Wakeman shares a joke with the players, while Pat Kruse pulls a face behind his back!

Dodgin's Destroyers includes the name of P. Kruse in a very unusual team formation

nightclub and there were one or two occasions that make you glad that the national press weren't so hot on football player exposés back then. I admit there were a few things that went on that we shouldn't be proud of and I was probably the worst in the side for wanting a beer after training.

We used the New Inn a lot and we knew the landlord, Sean, and all the regulars by name. You could get anything you needed in that pub, radios, televisions, a side of beef, anything! But there was a good side to all the socialising we did. It should be remembered that it wasn't all the time, that we got promotion, and because most of us were so close, the team became a stronger unit. In any case Bill would have dropped us if he felt we were letting the side down or we weren't performing, no doubt about it.

We used to mingle a lot with the fans after the game too and most of them wouldn't shy away from telling us if they thought we'd had a bad game. I remember being ticked off a couple of times in the bar after a home game, so we felt accountable to the fans for how we'd performed. It was good to talk with supporters about the game, sharing their enjoyment if we'd won, or explaining why things had gone wrong if we'd lost. I thought it was healthy.

I understand that the current Brentford players aren't allowed to mingle with the fans in the bar after a match, that's wrong I think. After some home games the players would stay out with the fans most of the night and I've even crashed out on a Brentford fan's sofa after a big Saturday night out.

The more relaxed drink-driving law back then must have helped?

I'm not proud to have to admit that you're right, but it was a long time ago now and people's attitudes were different then. Five pints after a game, then a forty-five minute drive home isn't an option today.

Do you recall the mood in the camp before the start of the 1977-78 promotion campaign?

It wasn't any different to the season before really, we felt confident but not under any pressure. Bill was so relaxed and it rubbed off on us.

As promotion became more and more of a reality every game was approached exactly the same, we weren't given any points targets, and even if a team was down the other end of the league Bill would treat them with respect. But we knew that if we played our normal brand of flowing football we would beat them over the ninety minutes if we stuck to our task.

With just a handful of games to go we knew what was needed to finish the job off and we felt the pressure more, especially when Barry Tucker gave an own goal away which cost us dear at Southend over Easter. But we clinched our promotion spot shortly afterwards beating Darlington two-nil at home. I've still got a big picture on my wall at home of all the players drinking champagne in the bath after that game and an empty bottle of Moët as a reminder of a great day.

Did the players wonder what was going on when the club decided to sell Gordon Sweetzer before promotion had been decided in 1978? He'd scored twelve goals in twenty matches, the sale must have jeopardized going up surely?

We did think it was a bit strange yes, but I'm not sure that Sweetzer fitted the bill as far as Dodgin was concerned, he was a bit too gung-ho for his liking at times I think.

Okay, he got goals, but Bill was looking for somebody more refined I think, so the manager must have thought Cambridge's £30,000 offer was too tempting and the money would allow him to buy someone else. But he didn't!

Brentford beat Swansea one-nil at Griffin Park on February 10th 1979. I don't expect you to remember the game, but if Brentford had lost or played really badly that day, I doubt I'd be here right now. That was my first ever Bees game and I've been addicted ever since, are you quite aware what you and your team-mates are responsible for and the suffering you've caused for me over the years?

[Laughs] I've got no apologies to make at all, no! Brentford Football Club is wonderful, perhaps they haven't been ruthless enough over the years, but you support one of the best clubs around.

Many Brentford fans consider the 1977-78 team as their favourite of all time, what do you think of that?

It makes me proud to be honest, along with the other members of that squad, it's lovely to be remembered like that.

There was a youngster by the name of Bob Booker emerging in your era who turned out to be a real Bees hero. What did you think of Bob?

Well I used to pick Bob up and give him a lift to and from training every day from Watford, so I got to know him and his family really well. I'll have to put my hand up and admit that I didn't think the tall, gangly youngster would go on to become as good as he did.

At the time my assessment was that he could be good but he didn't have the drive in him to get to the top, but I was wrong wasn't I? He looked an awkward player who didn't know his best position, but his move to Sheffield United helped him play in the top flight and I admire him for it. I also remember Bob scoring a hat-trick on his debut in the game we won seven-two against Hull City.

Until recently there was still some graffiti on a wall in Brentford that read 'Why sack Dodgin?' What's your answer to that?

Well I think it was decided that because we were struggling at the end of the 1979-80 season, more steel was needed from the man in charge to make sure we stayed up and to take the club forwards. The Board knew all about Fred Callaghan, so did the players, so they felt that he was the natural replacement. Some of Bill's signings late on left a lot to be desired too, for example replacing Andy McCulloch with Tony Funnell. [Laughs] If Bill was here today I think he'd admit to that being a real faux pas, a real 'hang your head in shame' signing. [Laughs] Tony Funnell!

Brentford stayed up thanks to a one-nil win against Millwall on the last day of the season, which was one of only a handful Funnell scored. But at the start of the following campaign a lot of players refused to sign new contracts for Fred Callaghan, was that an indication of unrest in the camp?

Yes, very much so. Fred came in and wanted to make lots of changes and it was unsettling from a player's point of view. Ron Harris was installed as his assistant, now, his is another name that always makes me laugh out loud! I would say that he contributed nothing, and when you consider the amount of years he'd been involved in football at a very, very high level, you would have thought he would be able to pass something positive on to the players, but he had no idea whatsoever. To be honest he couldn't string three sentences together and if you asked him for advice about something he just didn't have a clue or started swearing. Bringing Ron in was a very bad move on Fred's part.

Due to a long term injury to Jim McNichol and a contract dispute with Danis Salman, Callaghan decided to bring in Mark Hill and Iori Jenkins, were they any good as defenders do you think?

Mark Hill was a nice chap, but I didn't really rate him as a defender, not overly committed and not that skilful really. Jenkins was nothing to write home about either. To be honest as they were coming into the side, and although I was still being picked, I didn't really feel part of the team any more, things had changed for the worse in my view.

I remember going over to Yugoslavia for a pre-season tour and not being picked to start in some of the matches and I felt my time was coming to an end at the club. Fred then bought Alan Whitehead from Bury for £65,000 at the start of the 1981-82 season and I went out on loan to Northampton after a couple of games as substitute.

I only played one more game for Brentford, at Reading when Gordon Sweetzer made a surprise return from Canada, he scored but we lost four-one. But I guess my time was up, I'd gone from Player of the Year for 1979-80 to not part of the plans at twenty-eight. But that's football.

So it was Barry Fry who put you off playing football?
Kind of, yes. I disliked playing for him so much that I realised I was carrying on playing just for the sake of still being a 'footballer'. I knew I'd have to get a job away from the game sooner or later, so I called it a day and became a builder.

Have you been back to Brentford often since leaving?
Apart from the Griffin Park Centenary reunion hardly at all really, which is a shame because the place played a big part in my life for a few years. I bought tickets to go and see Brentford play Crewe at Wembley a few years back and it was nice to get recognised still and chat with some of fans, the team played really badly though.

One of my daughters had a ballet lesson at Covent Garden recently so I decided to kill a couple of hours and get the train out to Brentford. I had a quick pint in the New Inn for old times sake, then went back to pick her up.

1972: Frank Blunstone [black briefcase] with his promoted team before flying out to Guernsey

Frank Blunstone

Sandwiched in between the managerial reigns of Jimmy Sirrel and Mike Everitt, Frank Blunstone brought new hope to Bees fans that were sadly becoming used to life in the Fourth Division and the threat of re-election at the end of every season. It was a turbulent era, the club had witnessed a take-over bid from Queen's Park Rangers, a move that would have seen our club go out of existence, but against a dire financial backdrop, Blunstone managed to successfully manipulate one of the smallest squads in football history and start to turn fortunes around. With a handful of excellent signings, Frank led the club to promotion from the basement in 1972, and in doing so, brought the fans flooding back through the turnstiles at Griffin Park.

Frank had big plans for the club, his enthusiasm and valuable contacts could have been used to see Brentford resurrected as a leading London club again, but the perpetual lack of ambition from the Chairman of the day eventually took its toll when the former Chelsea Champion strolled off to Old Trafford where he became Tommy Docherty's assistant at Manchester United.

Frank is an fascinating man and his warmth and enthusiasm make him one of the most genuine and sincere people I think I've met. It is no exaggeration to say that I could have easily sat and listened to Frank's football reminiscing for days. Capped five times for England and one of the all time Stamford Bridge legends, Frank had a tough upbringing in Cheshire. One of fourteen children the former Crewe Alexandra starlet learned his playing skills the hard way, as he explains.

"From the age of about nine I used to have to work in the Cattle Market with all my family on Saturday mornings, and after washing down all the cows and rubbing them down with sawdust, all the men and boys used to have a big football match. They were real battles, hard, dirty and bruising, but as a kid you learned to look after yourself and toughen up, which I expect prepared me for my life as a professional footballer. These ding-dong games used to go on for an hour while the cattle dried and I remember being sent crashing into big, iron cattle-pens - my uncles simply told me to get up and get on with the game. When I arrived at Chelsea I was tough enough."

Frank's biggest achievements in the game undoubtedly occurred away from Brentford, but he still talks abut the club with a great deal of warmth and affection. Looking back, guiding Brentford to promotion in 1971-72 was a truly remarkable achievement given the circumstances, but then again, Frank Blunstone is a truly remarkable man.

What was it about Brentford that made you apply for the Manager's job?

Albert Sewell, the stats guy the presenters joke about on Match of the Day and Grandstand, told me that there was a job going at Brentford and I thought I'd apply for it – he wrote the programme for Chelsea at the time.

The Brentford job was only the second manager's job that I'd put my name forward for. I'd had a nightmare interview for the Reading position once when I was completely unprepared, but I did well enough to be given a chance at Griffin Park and I think I did well at the club. John Bond, who went on to take Norwich to the top flight, was also in the running for the Brentford job then.

It was quite a difficult time to have taken over at the club, we'd just fought off a take-over by QPR, the club were heavily in debt and there were only a handful of players on the books?
When I took over in 1968 we were £69,000 in the red and everything was cut back to the bare bones. I remember for one game I had to name goalkeeper Gordon Phillips as sub, that was when you were only allowed one sub and you were only allowed to use them if you had an injury. But I simply didn't have any more outfield players to bring in, I had to ask Gordon to sit on the bench.

But with Chic Brodie in goal I guess that there was always a good chance he'd get crocked, he was jinxed injury-wise wasn't he?
Oh Charlie, yes, he didn't have a lot of luck did he? I'm still asked about that game at Colchester when that dog ran onto the pitch and collided with him. I remember that incident really well actually, we were fighting near the top of the division and were doing quite well.

It was just before half time, with the scores still nil-all, and we were keeping possession really well. Then all of a sudden this dog came running onto the field and started chasing the ball around. As the ball was passed from player to player the dog set off and tried to chase it, we had about three or four passes, then the ball was played back to Alan Hawley on the half-way line.

He turned round and played the ball back to Charlie Brodie and as he bent down to pick the ball up the dog collided with him, the animal ran straight at him and its head smashed right into the side of Charlie's knee and did his ligaments.

He had to be carried off and in the end we lost four-nil. I gave the referee a right mouthful, he should have blown the whistle as soon as the dog ran on.

That wasn't the only time he picked up strange injuries was it?
No unfortunately, before that we were playing at Lincoln and Charlie tipped a cross over the bar – this big centre-forward came running in, missed the ball and Charlie, grabbed the net, then pulled it really hard in frustration. The crossbar collapsed and hit Charlie on the head! It knocked him straight out. There was about twenty minutes to go and we were losing one-nil, so I said to the referee, "you'll have to abandon the game..."

Frank Blunstone and Eddie Lyons in the dug-out

He refused and told the ground staff to go and find another goal. Unfortunately Lincoln had a practise field next to their ground and there was another goal there, but it had been in the ground for years and they couldn't get the thing out. So I went back to the referee and said, "look, we can't play on now, we'll have to cancel the match."

He told us all to go back to the dressing rooms and wait, then, about a quarter of an hour later, they managed to replace the cross bar - but it was so crooked it was ridiculous. I told to the referee that we couldn't play on because the bar wasn't straight, but he insisted we finished the game.

I was trying to get the game called off because we were losing, but he wasn't having any of it! Then there was the time that somebody in the crowd threw a fake hand-grenade at Charlie while were playing Millwall!

You had three mixed seasons at Brentford, but in difficult circumstances, you did a fair job didn't you?

Yes we did, the first two years were very good, we got promoted, and then got relegated again straight away – but that was the Chairman Les Davey's fault.

The Cup run was good too, we went to Cardiff who were top of the Second Division at the time and beat them two-nil, before going out at Hull City in the Fifth Round in front of almost 40,000. But we should have got something out of that game, one of their goals was a foul on the 'keeper and should have been disallowed. We had some good crowds at Griffin Park then too, we had 18,000 against Crewe Alexandra – that season we averaged almost 12,000 and got the financial deficit right down. The season we went down though, I knew it was on the cards.

Why do you say that?

Well the Chairman didn't have a clue. He came up to me once and asked why we didn't have better players and when I told him why, because he wouldn't pay decent wages or transfers, he didn't like it. He wouldn't even give the players a rise when they won promotion.

Because of that, at the start of the following season, only six of them had signed a contract to play, so I had a major problem. I was always falling out with Davey, we almost lost Stuart Houston because of the board, they just wouldn't pay out for anything. Dave Sexton at Chelsea did me a massive favour by telling me about Houston.

John O'Mara had been banned for five games by the Football League because of his poor disciplinary record and we needed a replacement if we wanted to go up, but the idiot Chairman said we couldn't have one.

Eric Radley-Smith, the old club doctor, gave me the money out of his own pocket to pay Houston's signing on fee in the end, that is the only reason we got the player and won promotion that season.

Stuart Houston was a great signing, didn't you sign John Docherty too?

Yes, I got him from £250 from my old Chelsea captain, Roy Bentley, from Reading. I got Paul Bence from there too. The best deal I did while I was at Brentford, though, was buying John O'Mara, I'd been watching him for ages. He was 6ft 3inches tall, big built, but didn't have a clue about the game. But for £800 I knew I'd be able to do something with him.

I put so much training in with O'Mara, coaching him myself and taught him the game and how to make good runs. He got twenty-eight goals for me, but he got booked almost as often as he scored! He was quick too, I entered him into the professional footballer's athletics meeting at Wimbledon Dog Track just after he arrived and he came through all the heats and came second in the eighty metres. For a big guy I thought that was fantastic.

Then Brentford flogged him!

Brentford would sell anyone. Ken Furphy was manager at Blackburn at the time and straight after we'd beaten them four-nil at Griffin Park he came up to me and asked if I'd sell John.

I laughed and said knowing the Chairman I expect so. He rang back on the Monday morning and offered £30,000 for John and he went, but he never scored a goal for them! But I knew how to deal with O'Mara, I knew how to wind him up to get the best out of him.

Roger Cross was another one of yours too wasn't he?

Yes, Ron Greenwood at West Ham did me a favour with Cross, he let me have him for £10,000 because he didn't really need him, although he was a very good player, he still had Martin Peters and Geoff Hurst.

Roger wasn't the bravest in the area, but he was good on the ball and worked well with O'Mara and Little Doc - it was a lovely blend. Then one day Bill Dodgin rang me up and asked if I'd sell Roger Cross, so I had to say those words again, "I expect so, Brentford will sell anybody!"

I wanted to sign Stan Bowles from Crewe too, I could have had him for £15,000 cash, but there's no way the Chairman would have paid that, the same with Andy McCulloch who was at QPR at the time — we had the money from O'Mara and I thought he would have been the perfect replacement.

How do you remember the club and the fans at Brentford?

They were brilliant, I loved Brentford, I had four very enjoyable years there. I wouldn't have left Brentford. I had the chance of going to Everton which I turned down, Tommy Docherty kept phoning me to go to Manchester United and I turned him down twice. But in the end the Chairman refused to become more ambitious and I decided to go to Old Trafford. I just couldn't continue working in those conditions and I simply couldn't get on with him – everything was always a struggle.

But I really liked the club and that was part of the reason I came back to Griffin Park to help Fred Callagan when he was manager, we had some good players then, Terry Hurlock, Chris Kamara, Stan Bowles, Francis Joseph, Paddy Roche. I've had some good times at Brentford."

There's talk of Brentford moving out of Griffin Park into a new stadium, how important do you think it is for the club to stay in its hometown?

I think it's very important, but I think you should have been able to stay at Griffin Park. The trouble is that Martin Lange kept selling off parts of the ground and building flats on them. You could have re-built a lovely ground on Griffin Park.

CULT BEES AND LEGENDS VOLUME TWO

Richard Cadette

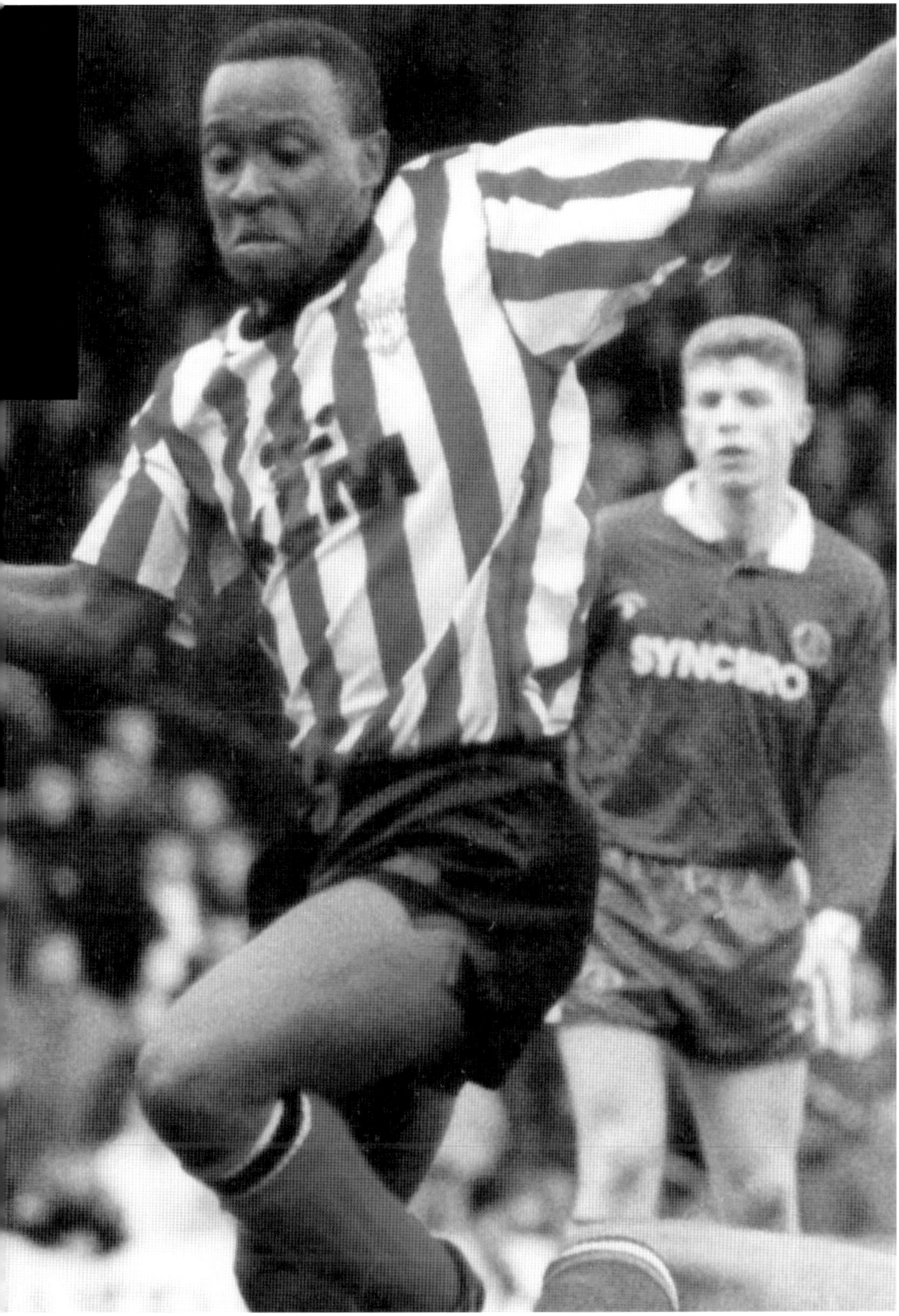
SYNCHRO

Oooh Richard Cadette, Oooh Richard Cadette, Oooh Richard Cadette in the back of the net, Yeah! I used to love hearing that song reverberating around Griffin Park in the late 80s and early 90s as the Brentford centre-forward scored a goal in his pin-striped red and white centenary season kit.

Signed for £77,500 from Sheffield United by Steve Perryman, Tricky Dicky became an overnight hit with the Brentford fans. His close ball skills and blistering pace off the blocks gave the side a really dynamic cutting edge, and until the arrival of Dean Holdsworth, the Blissett-Cadette partnership provided goals-a-plenty and the first genuine indication that promotion out of Division Three was becoming a distinct possibility.

Many fans will vividly remember the way Cadette used to hold up the ball using his low centre of gravity. Back to goal, holding off a defender, he'd then either twist and turn on goal using the trademark drop of the shoulder, or lay the ball off for Blissett to rifle home. Cadette ended the 1988-89 season as the club's top scorer with seventeen goals, many of which were set up by himself using that fantastic burst of speed.

On his day Richard Cadette was awesome I thought and after his departure, groups of Brentford fans suffering from withdrawal symptoms, myself included, made pilgrimages up to Falkirk so they could get a Cadette fix.

Richard had several successful seasons under Jim Jeffries at Brockville Park with Falkirk and was one of the highest scorers in the Scottish Premier League while he was north of the border. Richard eventually moved back to London, finishing his professional playing days with Millwall.

Cadette is now attempting to climb the football management ladder, and with the help of former Bees team mate Keith Jones as right hand man at Tooting and Mitcham, the duo are building a good reputation for themselves.

Can you talk us through your move from Sheffield United to Brentford?
To be honest I was really happy that Steve Perryman came in for me. I wanted to get away from Sheffield because I knew the kind of football that was going to be played by Dave Bassett and I wasn't about to start chasing long balls into the corners for anybody. I was born in Hammersmith so I knew about the club, but to be truthful the only reason I really agreed to join was the fact that Perryman was in charge.

So you had a lot of respect for Steve Perryman from his playing days?
Yeah, I thought I could only become a better player by coming and being coached by somebody like Steve. It wasn't the fact that it was Brentford that were in for me, it was definitely because Steve Perryman was involved that persuaded me to sign.

So he didn't have to give Brentford the hard sell to you?

Well, he did have to tell me about his plans and the kind of team he was putting together. I'd played at Brentford with Southend United, and to be honest I wasn't overly impressed, but Steve told me all about Andy Sinton, Keith Jones, Gary Blissett and that he was about to sign Tony Parks from Spurs, so it seemed to be a club on the move.

You were brought in to link up with Gary Blissett and make the forward line a lot more dynamic, how did you view your partnership?

I don't think Blissett had scored that many goals in the season before I joined, he certainly hadn't become as prolific as he was over the next couple of seasons at that stage. I knew he was good in the air and had a good touch, then during the pre-season when I first arrived, we started to click.

I was able to read his game and I saw how he positioned himself when I got the ball, he would lurk on the edge of the area. I knew that if I got the ball to my feet I could attack the box then roll it back towards Bliss, I would be able to find him. He was a good target man.

To be honest we made good partners and we scored a lot of goals together. Gary was a good geezer, a good player on the pitch, and a good laugh off it.

Perryman had a lot of attacking options in that side to support you and Blissett. Neil Smillie, Keith Jones, Alan Cockram and Andy Sinton all loved to get forward too. Did you rate that side?

Yes, when you look at the squad we had some great players for that level. You only have to look at the teams we beat in the 1988-89 Cup run to realise that although we were a very good team on our day, what killed us was the small squad. It was good, but not big enough to cope with all those matches. Then as soon as we got knocked out of the FA Cup at Liverpool Andy Sinton was sold, which weakened us even more. You can't blame Andy for leaving though, if you get a chance to play at the top level, you take it.

Did the Cup run surprise the players as much as it did the media?

Not really, you never expect to get to the Quarter Finals obviously, but if you're in a good team and form is on your side then those one-off cup-ties can really work out well. Getting Peterborough and Walsall back to our place and turning them over in replays were the really tricky matches, after those we relaxed more.

I knew we would beat Manchester City, I think a lot of the fans did too, there was something about the atmosphere where people could sense an upset was on the cards, but in some respects it wasn't really an upset as we outplayed them. The same at Blackburn in the Fifth Round, we knew we could turn them over too, we'd played them in the League Cup earlier in the season and they robbed us. We went out six-five on aggregate, but we really scared them, so again, I knew we'd win at Ewood Park. We played better football against teams from a higher division for sure, we knew we could play and we stepped up a gear.

I take it you weren't quite so confident at Anfield?
Against any other club left in the Quarter Finals I would have been, but Liverpool were special then, a similar calibre to Arsenal today. If English teams had been allowed to play in Europe at that time I think they would have been European Champions, they were quality. John Barnes, John Aldridge, Steve McMahon, Alan Hansen, Peter Beardsley, Ronnie Whelan, Ray Houghton, Gary Gillespie, Kenny Dalglish as manager, quality.

But we had Andy Feeley!
[Laughs] You're right, we did, we did have Andy Feeley.

Obviously I wouldn't be doing my job unless I asked you about your miss, the one that you could have scored at The Kop end to put Brentford one-nil up. Does it haunt you as much as it does us?
[Grins] I knew you'd mention that, but it was hardly a sitter and just went past the post. Well, I think of it this way, if we had taken the lead I think it would have really rattled Liverpool's cage, they probably would have scored eight or nine after going a goal behind. It would have made them a lot more angry, earlier.

We really missed Simon Ratcliffe at Anfield, he would have tightened things up and perhaps Liverpool would have had a tougher time breaking us down. Simon was strong, he would have got his foot in.

A very young Marcus Gayle made his debut that season, what did the players make of him as a raw, skinny youngster?
Marcus always had ability, but as you say, he was just raw and struggled early on. He had some tough times in those early days I remember, but the other players recognised his potential and were as helpful as they could be, although we did call him 'Arfur', 'Arfur Lung'. I remember in one game against Birmingham where he was brought on as sub, then was subbed himself late on because he was so knackered. I think he was suffering from a few growing problems, he used to cramp up, but what really sorted him out was going away to Scandinavia for the close season.

He left like a twig and he came back all muscles, really pumped up. I used to bring him in to training and I remember picking him up the first day back after the summer and saying, "Marcus, have you been on those steroids mate?"

1990: Richard Cadette celebrates with the Brentford fans after scoring at Fulham

He hadn't even been doing weights, and he told me that he just ached all over from simply growing, I don't know what they fed him on over there! But in the early days he had the right attitude, he'd take the stick, listen to the advice, absorb it all, and it paid off... He's had a great career.

What did you think of Perryman as a manager?

The first year I thought he was different class, I was learning things from him and I was really enjoying playing for him. The second season he went to pot I think, he gave Phil Holder too much of a say, and what Holder had to say was crap. I think Holder had a very negative effect. Keith Jones played for Perryman when Mickey Hazzard was helping him at Brentford and says they made a far better combination. I think we stopped passing the ball as much after Holder arrived, we were lashing it up the field more often and that's just not enjoyable in my eyes.

Did Holder confuse Perryman's 'stylish football' philosophy?

Yes, especially after Dean Holdsworth signed, it seemed as if Perryman was getting impatient and changed his plans and how he wanted his side to play. John Buttegieg is the perfect example, he was easily the best player at the club, too good for Brentford.

But because the players who were expected to play alongside Buttegieg in a sweeper system weren't capable of adapting, it got shelved. It was probably around then that Steve decided he might not be able to 'play' his way out of the division after all. But if I wanted to play long-ball football I would have stayed at Sheffield.

But that style of football saw us through to the play-offs against Tranmere in 1991, then under Holder, to promotion.

The play-off season was a frustrating season for me, I was injured for a chunk of the campaign and I think we should have been stronger in the league. The squad was certainly better I thought, the head-count was up too, it was a big disappointment to go out in the play-offs. So near, yet so far.

Did you realise that Holdsworth's arrival would have such a big effect on your chances at Brentford?

Steve was really good about it to be fair, he called me in a couple of times to go through why he was bringing in another striker, he said he needed to have more competition up front and you can't ask for more than that from your manager. Being honest and up front is the best way to be, exactly the way I try to be with my team now that I am in management. No disrespect to Deano or Bliss but I knew I had a lot more in my bag than they did, but for whatever reason, things don't always work out.

Reading between the lines, I take it that Phil Holder wasn't as open and honest with you?

No, and that pissed me off to be honest. I'd have preferred it if Phil had just called me to one side and told me that he didn't rate me. Another thing that didn't help were those silly rumours that started to circulate from the club that I was a troublemaker, what bollocks. That's just not me at all, but when you hear those kind of things mysteriously springing up you know that it's time to be looking elsewhere. I just wasn't one of the yes-men that he'd surrounded himself with, that's what you needed to be to really get on with Phil I think.

Was the whole Perryman departure saga as much of a shock to the players as it was to the fans?

I don't think so, I wasn't too surprised, Steve had started to get itchy feet maybe. I think he was getting frustrated that there wasn't the funding in place at Brentford to be able to really take the club forward. Martin Lange had allowed some decent players to be brought in to be fair, but I think he wanted to see results before taking things to the next level. I thought things had gone downhill quickly at Brentford, then as soon as Perryman left, well, it was time for me to go too.

Even though the management stopped picking you for whatever reason, the fans never lost faith in Richard Cadette did they?

The fans were always really good to me at Brentford, [smiles] but then supporters are always good to strikers who score goals aren't they? If you put the ball in the back of the net often enough all fans are going to love you. I just wished we could have got into the play-offs after the FA Cup run, I think if we'd have gone up that season things could have been very different for Brentford Football Club now, especially under Perryman. The fixture backlog and the Mickey Mouse Cup run cost us dear, there were too many games at the end of the season, and it was impossible to keep the momentum going.

Falkirk came in for you, that must have been a bit of a bolt from the blue?

Going to Falkirk to play for Jim Jeffries was a great move for me, I did well up there and had a great time. It was like living inside a goldfish bowl up there, everyone knows everyone, they're lovely people too and so passionate about football. The transfer came along at just the right time for me, looking back, getting out of England was possibly the best thing I could have done as a footballer. I really, really enjoyed my time in Scotland, I went up for a year and ended up staying three.

CULT BEES AND LEGENDS VOLUME TWO

Jackie Graham

Hard as nails Jackie Graham was the archetypal 70s midfield Scottish terrier. Never afraid to roll his sleeves up and get stuck in for the cause, never giving less than 100% in the red and white stripes of Brentford and never to be forgotten. Jackie's impressive attitude to the game ensured that if Brentford were to go down, they'd go down battling, and over the years, Brentford fans have learned that spirit is well worth celebrating.

Jackie joined Brentford via Dundee and Guildford City in 1970. The Bees pipped a host of other league clubs to the signature of the goal-scoring midfielder, and what superb value for money he provided over the next decade. Ten sterling years service were notched up at Griffin Park, although most of those years were spent in Division Four, Jackie won promotion under two different Bees managers and showed the kind of passion that has cemented his position in the club's hall of fame. You ask any Brentford fan who was a regular at Griffin Park during the 1970s about Jackie Graham and all you will here back are superlatives.

Jackie's less than acrimonious departure from Griffin Park under Fred Callaghan's management was regrettable after all the player had given the club, but he still looks back at his time at Brentford with immense pride. Like many other players from that era, Graham made friends for life while at Griffin Park and recorded some fantastic memories from a great football career at our club.

Jackie currently runs an office cleaning business in Guildford and is currently adapting to life as a Grandad.

How did a young lad with such a broad Scottish accent end up playing for Guildford City... Can you tell us about your early years?

Well, I was born in Glasgow and was raised a big Rangers fan, I went to a lot of games at Ibrox as a kid, so I was a real football fan before I became a professional player. In fact I still get up there to see one or two games a season, Walter Smith, who was a team-mate at my first club Dundee United, went on to be the manager at Rangers, so he sorts me out with tickets from time to time.

After leaving school I got the chance to sign at Tannadice but I never really got on too well with the United manager, Gerry Kerr. The problem was that I always wanted to get back to Glasgow to see my mates - he wanted me to live full time in Dundee. We were always falling out over that but I still spent five years at the club. I had to stay in digs, a massive, run-down old mansion house that the club owned, which was a complete nightmare for a single guy.

I don't think Gerry liked Glasgow lads very much, I got the impression he thought all we wanted to do was drink and lark about... [Laughs] He was right, the Glasgow boys in the side used to cause mayhem! I had enough of it all up there in the end, so as my girlfriend lived in Guildford, I decided to come down for a bit of an extended holiday. I fancied getting away from Dundee for a while, that was in 1969 when I was twenty-two, I've been here ever since. I love the City.

Guildford City Football Club signed me and I also found a local job, although I must admit I didn't really turn up that often and made do with the appearance money from the football. Guildford used to get some cracking crowds and the players used to get an attendance bonus, so the money was okay. I must have done pretty well because it wasn't long before other clubs started coming in for me, but I chose Brentford.

Frank Blunstone was the Bees manager who signed you but what other clubs were in competition for your signature?

Well Guildford were holding out to get the maximum they could for me, which eventually meant that I was getting mucked about quite a bit by the club and the situation became very annoying for me.

Every week I was being called in by the manager and told that this club or that club wanted to sign me, then just as it looked as if I was about to go, Guildford would up the money and the deals fell through.

I got keyed up so many times to move; Wolves, Oxford, Cardiff, Coventry and Leeds all pulled out because of the way Guildford were acting, so in the end I thought screw them. Off my own back I got a mate of mine to drive me to Brentford and signed. I didn't even negotiate wages, I just wanted to get back to playing full-time football.

The Guildford City officials went absolutely potty when they found out, but there was nothing they could do. Brentford paid them something, but it would have been peanuts compared to what some of the other clubs had offered and I moved into a club house in Hounslow.

I didn't regret making that trip because Frank Blunstone was very good for me, I had a great deal of respect for the man and he helped me develop as a footballer.

So Blunstone became the first of five Brentford managers you played under, what did you make of him?

Frank was great, absolutely brilliant I thought and he opened my eyes quite a bit by what he taught me. I was playing up front at inside-left for Guildford and had scored quite a few goals from that position, a similar position to Frank's at Chelsea when they'd won the First Division Championship, so he was able to pass on lots to me.

He helped me think about my strengths and weaknesses as a player and we came to the conclusion that perhaps I should be used more as a central midfielder, which worked well and I established myself there over the next few years. Frank used to lay on some good training sessions I thought and he was a very good coach. If he'd got some more backing from the chairman he could have achieved a lot at Brentford.

After being frustrated at Dundee United and Guildford did you enjoy life at Griffin Park in those early days?
Aye, I did, I palled up with fellow Scot Dick Renwick who was the Brentford left-back. I knew him a bit from before I joined Brentford, I'd bumped into him at Guildford a couple of times, he lived in Aldershot and would pop in now and again. He was a hard man, one of the hardest I've ever seen.

Dick knew everything about the game and he was a brilliant man to listen to, but Jesus was he tough. During a season some players count how many goals they've scored or helped set up, others count how many clean sheets they've helped keep, Dick used to count how many stitches he'd put into people. Seriously!

He sounds like one of those players that fans love if they're on your side, but hate if he's with the opposition?
Exactly, he used to get a hostile reception at some grounds because of what had happened in previous games. During the warm-up up at Chester when I first arrived the crowd were shouting all kinds of things at him, I could hear people screaming, "Oi Renwick you ginger ****", and that was just during the warm-up! I later found out that he'd broken the legs of two different players the last time he'd played there.

It must be said that although Blunstone's sides could play a bit, there were some real hard-men in that side, you couldn't have taken too many prisoners at the time?
Well at the back with Dick Renwick was Peter Gelson and Alan Nelmes who were also both hard men. Nelmsie is often thought of as being a more gentle player, but he would kick you as good as anyone, just more subtly and not get booked for it. Gelson was a great tackler, so strong in the air too, a marvellous player. At right-back was Alan Hawley, he was just class I thought, one of the best tacklers I ever played with.

Just as a player thought they had got past him, Hawley would come sliding in, he had a brilliant knack. Up front was John O'Mara, or 'Big Ted' as I call him, he's still a big mate of mine... Ted was my regular drinking buddy. Frank Blunstone put in a lot of extra work with John O'Mara and we were always doing extra sessions, Frank and myself would cross ball after ball into the area for O'Mara to head, and look how it paid off. He was absolutely brilliant at that level.

Was there a pecking order of hardness in that side?
Oh Dick was definitely the hardest player at the club, possibly the hardest player at any club. He was so solid and even in training, if you went in for a tackle with him he'd hammer you! You cringed before the challenge was made and he intimidated some players. I never saw anyone ever square up to Dick after a game either, no matter what had happened in a game he would always be the first one at the bar, home or away, ordering his pint of light and bitter.

He couldn't run, so I played in front of him and did all that for him, he often said that my legs helped him stay in the game an extra two seasons. We still keep in touch from time to time, but he lives up near Burnley now so it's difficult.

It's a widely held view that the 1970s featured the toughest men ever to play the game at a professional level, would you say that was true or a bit of an urban myth?
I'd say it was probably true, you certainly had to be able to look after yourself. The rules hadn't been too messed around with at that stage, you'd get locked up these days for some of the things that went on during a match back then. When you went up to places like Workington, Barrow, Scunthorpe and Bradford you knew you were in for a battle. You had to have your sleeves rolled up ready for a fight. You knew who would 'play' for Brentford at places like those, and there were enough of us in the side who were prepared to do what was required.

Wearing the Brentford shirt with pride always goes down well with the fans, perhaps that's why some of the names from your era are still talked about in the pubs on match-days even today. The 70's coincided with the most unsuccessful era in the club's history, but some of the biggest terrace heroes played at the same time. Why do you think that is?
I think it's because the backbone of that side would go out and sweat blood for the club, they really would. Fans and players from some of those northern sides probably thought we would be southern softies, in fact I remember being called it on more than one occasion, so I had to remind them of my Glasgow origins! There were maybe one or two players who may not have had that extra 'steel', but they soon got found out, and they're not worth talking about really.

With so many strong characters in the dressing room did Frank Blunstone ever struggle to keep the discipline?
Frank was a great coach, but maybe not so good at man-management. I remember after we won promotion in 1971-72 we went on an end of

season tour to Guernsey. Before we went he told us all to go over there and relax, to enjoy the break, but I don't think he was prepared for the amount of drinking that went on. Myself and Big Ted [John O'Mara], plus a fair few others, were at the bar morning, noon and night.

He didn't mention it at the time, but at the beginning of the next season, at our wage negotiation meetings, he pulled us up on it and only gave us a small increase. We may have liked our beer, but we were both among the hardest trainers at the club too.

Frank wasn't a drinker so I guess he couldn't understand footballers that did. In fact I only ever saw Frank Blunstone with a whole pint in his hand once, that was at Eddie Lyons' funeral, we all raised our glasses and had a drink for Eddie that day.

A trip to the Channel Islands as a reward for promotion seems very modest in this day and age?

[Laughs] It felt pretty modest back then too! I hate travelling by plane so I got the train down to Weymouth with the club doctor and director, Radley-Smith, he was another nice man.

We caught the boat over to Guernsey from there. It was a bit of a drawn-out way of getting over, but the boat had a bar, so it wasn't too much of a hardship!

A week in Guernsey may not have been the icing on the cake you had hoped for, but winning promotion must have felt fantastic?

We played really well that season and there was a feeling in the camp that I never felt again, we knew we could go out and win every match. At certain stages that season the players used to talk openly about how many goals we thought we'd get in the next game, it didn't seem arrogant, we just had such a belief in our team.

And that's the way it was, we used to score four or five goals regularly and bagged six goals in three separate matches that season. Winning all the time is a great feeling.

Frank had us playing to a system that we all knew inside out, the defenders knew where to play the ball to the midfield and we knew where to play the ball in to the forwards, who in turn knew where to run to receive a pass. It was slick. We could play blindfolded and know how to pick out a team-mate and we played a lot of nice football under Frank.

John Docherty was still a good little player, very lively out on the wing and he had a couple of tricks up he sleeve. Some may have thought that Doc was a bit selfish at times, but most Jocks are! He knew how to lose his marker and whip in a dangerous cross for 'Big Ted', there was a really good mixture in that team.

You scored the final Brentford goal of the 1971-72 promotion season, our third in a three-nil win at Barrow, do you remember it?

I remember missing the train back to London after the game more! John O'Mara, Gordon Phillips, Alan Hawley and myself decided to go walk-about after the game. We'd arranged to meet the rest of the lads at the station but we decided to stay up there for the night and go out on the town.

We heard that Frank Blunstone was pacing up and down the platform waiting for us until the last second, and we got our arses kicked by him when we turned up for training on the Monday.

People are always talking about the sales of John O'Mara, Roger Cross and Stewart Houston and the impact they had on the club, but not all of our best players left the club. You stayed for ten years, surely you must have had opportunities to move on to a bigger club too?

You're right, there were a few clubs that came in for me while I was at Brentford. I remember Frank Blunstone calling me in to his office once to tell me that he had two offers for me and to ask me if I wanted to leave Brentford? I asked him if he wanted me to leave.

He said, "no Jackie, I want you to stay, I want to build a team around you..." So that was it, I stayed, and Frank promised to sort me out with a wage rise at the end of the season. I shouldn't have held my breath though, five quid a week extra was all I was given. "Thanks a fucking lot boss", I said to him, "is that what you call sorting me out?"

He then buggered off to Manchester United and I was left on £30 a week! We still joke about that whenever we see each other. I was gutted that Frank left, it was then that I really wished that he'd sold me when those offers came in.

How good was Stewart Houston in your view?

Very good, in fact better than good. He was another close friend of mine, the Scottish connection helped I guess, and we used to take it in turns to go round to each other's houses for Sunday lunch.

He had pace and ability, whether it be at left-back or in midfield, he had a good left peg too. He was too good for Brentford to be honest and it was no surprise when a bigger club snapped him up.

I remember the look on his face when he found out that he was going to play for Manchester United, he was completely and utterly stunned... Can you imagine the equivalent of a Fourth Division player getting transferred to Old Trafford these days, but Frank Blunstone [who had moved to Manchester United as a coach by that stage] had obviously convinced United manager, Tommy Docherty, about his potential. Everyone knew he wouldn't be staying at Brentford, moving from Chelsea to Griffin Park was only ever going to be a stepping stone for Stewart and that's what it proved to be, we were all really pleased for him.

Fate would have it that Brentford got drawn in the League Cup to play against Stewart Houston's Manchester United at Old Trafford the season after he left, do you remember the trip?
Keith Lawrence headed us ahead from a Paul Bence free kick, one-up at Old Trafford! We deserved a draw from the match, but the goalie, Bill Glazier, messed it up for us on the night and we lost two-one.

At least you got a chance to play that night, the year before you missed out in the League Cup tie at Liverpool - did you travel up to watch the match anyway?
No I didn't go up there and watch. I'd been sent off the week before at Southport for fighting, we could have appealed against it I suppose, which would have allowed me to play, but I was guilty as charged and I would have ended up with an extended suspension if I'd wasted their time. It was more important I was available for the league matches.

Were you aware that there was boardroom talk about transferring you back to Guildford City at one stage?
Yeah I remember that, it was the year Mike Everitt was in charge, I was really hacked off because his arrival was a real kick in the goolies. I bumped into an ex-Guildford team-mate one night, who'd become manager after I left, and he told me how much he'd like to have me back at the club. I told him that if he could match my wages then I'd seriously consider it, and there were talks between the clubs, but nothing came of it in the end.

Brentford's fate after going up has been well documented during the interviews for these books, but what are your views on the team's relegation in 1973?
The lack of investment in the side obviously played a major part in what happened that season, but I thought we were really unlucky too. We played some great football that year in my view and it seemed as if we lost a lot of games just by the odd goal here and there, we seemed to get punished harshly for mistakes. The players that were brought in were too ordinary which didn't help either.

How much of an impact did the other big name sales have on the squad or did the players see their transfers as an incentive; if you played well you stood every chance of a top club coming in for you and Brentford not standing in your way?

The early days, Jackie Graham went on to become a true Brentford legend

The players certainly missed those guys and it did make you question where the club was really heading if they sell everyone half-decent. Brentford had more potential than the Watfords and Wimbledons of this world, but we stood still because of the club's selling policy, whereas the other clubs went on to far bigger and better things.

That shouldn't have been allowed to happen. Letting Frank Blunstone go and replacing him with Mike Everitt really pissed the players off, I liked Mike as a guy, but when he first arrived he really tried to rock the boat and it back-fired on him big-style.

Was Everitt's failure down to his lack of ability or didn't the players allow him to succeed?

Everitt was upsetting people left right and centre when he arrived, he'd shout at the players all week long in training then expect us to go out on a Saturday and play well for him. He showed a blatant disrespect for some players who had served the club really well, players like Peter Gelson.

Mike was completely out of his depth, big-time. I remember the first day he walked into the training ground and spoke to all the players, he was all done up in his smartest clobber; tight black trousers, a little thin tie and all his hair Brylcreemed back. A few of us had to stop ourselves laughing, we really did, and I heard one or two giggles from the back… His first words were, "you might want to call me Mike, or Mick, Mr. Everitt, or Guvnor…. maybe even Chief…", then he puffed his chest out and put his arms behind his back for extra effect… "No, you lot can call me BOSS!"

Again it was hard not to laugh, especially when the next morning he turned up with the letters B-O-S-S right across the front of his training top. Hilarious! If anyone ever tracks him down can they remind him that he still owes me £10.

Under Mike Everitt Brentford really slumped, and during the course of the 1973-74 season propped up the whole of the Football League. The league tables showed that we had become the worst team in the whole country. How did that feel?

Well we used to have staff meetings where Mike used to try and rally the troops, but no matter what he said we knew we weren't going anywhere with him in charge. We used to try and encourage the players in the side who normally kept their views to themselves to speak up, we'd go out and have a couple of beers and encourage them to open up and share what they really thought and some good came of it. But at the end of the day no matter how much endeavour players have, unless they can match it with ability you will still struggle. It was simple, as a team we got punished as often as we did because too many players weren't up to it.

Do you remember the players having to use their own cars to drive up for a match at Doncaster in 1974 when your coach failed to turn up?

Yeah I do, and we won too. I'm surprised the club didn't demand we drove ourselves to games every week after that! They could have saved a few more quid.

John Docherty took over as manager eventually, but things didn't really improve greatly. Did it seem strange having a former team-mate come back as a manager?

Doc and myself had a good relationship and we always used to go out for a couple of drinks after a game. But John was a 'pinickity wee fucker' he really was, he was like it as a player too, in fact when Doc moved to Queen's Park Rangers as a coach in 1974, all the other Brentford players went out on a piss-up to celebrate. He knows about that too! As manager he was very petty at times and upset quite a few of the lads on the training ground, but we got used to his style, but to be fair he was very knowledgeable about the game.

Docherty tried to re-sign John O'Mara to help revive his team's fortunes but the move didn't quite come off did it?

That's right he did try, well, it was a bit of a collective effort really. One Saturday night, just after I'd got home after a game, the phone went and it was Doc. He asked me if I was able to drive back to the club because he'd decided he wanted to try and bring O'Mara back to Griffin Park, at the time he was playing in South Africa.

So I went straight back to the ground and phoned him up, I said, "we need you back big man get yourself over here!" He told me that he'd just settled over in Africa and how difficult it would be to up sticks again and move straight back to England, but when I told him that if he didn't then Docherty was probably for the chop, he agreed. O'Mara told his South African club, packed up everything, flew home, just in time to hear that Dan Tana had sacked Doc! Would you believe it?

That put me in a very awkward situation, so as soon as Bill Dodgin arrived I went in and told him what had happened, he agreed to have a look at O'Mara with a view to signing him, but he chose to go after Andy McCulloch instead.

I remember Tana calling me up to his office to tell me that he'd sacked Doc, the chairman said, "after what he's just said to me I don't want that man back at this football club ever again!" I wanted to help iron the problem out and offered to have a word with Docherty, so I asked Tana to give me ten minutes to chat with Doc and smooth things over, but Tana wasn't having any of it.

1977: Jackie Graham meets the 'Brentford Popular Front' before a home match.

1978: Jackie Graham celebrates along with Pat Kruse, Stevie Phillips and Len Bond

Dan Tana's arrival as chairman seemed to coincide with a distinct upturn in Brentford's fortunes though, was this more than just coincidental in your view?

Dan was a real character and his big personality rubbed off on the players and the club I feel, maybe that alone helped pull the club out of the doldrums. He started to take the players out to all his favourite fancy restaurants and up to his barbers to get our hair cut… We'd never experienced anything like that before. Of course a few of the lads would abuse the wine list and it got a bit messy sometimes but Dan didn't mind because he knew it was all about bonding and Tana got a good response from the players I feel.

I remember we were playing up north one week, we lost the game although we played quite well, but Dan Tana decided to come over to the bar in our hotel that evening and have a little pop at Willie Graham who he obviously thought hadn't performed as well as he'd liked. Myself, Gordon Sweetzer and Willie Graham were standing at the hotel bar chatting, when over walked the chairman. He looked at Willie and said, "do you know what?" "No, what's that Chairman?" Willie replied… Tana went on to say, "You know when you get a woman back to your bedroom, you get her dress off…. Isn't that right Jackie?" "Aye Chairman, that's right, you get her dress off", I replied slightly puzzled. Tana added, "then you get her bra and knickers off, isn't that right Jackie?" "Aye Chairman" I smirked… Willie looked confused…. He went on "then what?... Then 'UMPH', but that's what you lack, you lack the final 'UMPH'!"

Sweetzer and I were crying with laughter, poor old Willie just didn't know where to look. Willie was a good lad, he used to come over to my house for dinner a fair bit for something to eat… Take my word, there are few things funnier in life than watching Willie Graham eating a plate of Spaghetti Bolognaise!

Bill Dodgin's arrival seemed to be really good news for you personally, you'd become a much respected senior pro at the club and Bill made you captain for the first time. Did you think being offered the captain's arm-band was a long-overdue gesture at Brentford?

John Docherty had offered me the captain's job before Bill but I didn't want it at the time, so I turned Doc down. I thought the players would resent the fact and assume it was just a 'Jock thing', that the manager was giving me preferential treatment because I was a fellow Scot. We spent a lot of time together though, and he confided most things in me, running ideas past me to see what I thought.

Bill Dodgin's arrival was a breath of fresh air. I once said that if Bill asked me to shoot somebody, I would. I meant it too, I just loved the man. I miss him today as much as I did when he first passed away, I really do. He was a player's manager, a real man's man, and under Dodgin it was nights out, red wine and golf-a-plenty! Some may say his ideas about the game were a bit old fashioned at the time, but I didn't see anything wrong with wanting to get the ball down and play.

Most of the training was based around five-a-sides to improve our close control and passing, Bill never made us do much running. It would often be the case that half way through a training session, when perhaps the lads weren't playing particularly well, Bill would call me over to tell the players to call it a day and get changed… "Tell them we're off to Foxhill Golf Course, they've all got to be there in one hour!"

The first thing Bill did for me when he arrived was to call me up to his office to go through my contract. He couldn't believe that my terms were so inferior to some of the others. That was my fault I guess because I never really made demands or jumped up and down over money in the time I'd been at Brentford, so he ripped it up in front of me and sorted me out. I got a loyalty bonus included for the first time, eight years after joining the club. Bill didn't have to do any of that.

You enjoyed playing for Bill so much that during one game you refused to come off when your number was held up to be substituted during the home match with Stockport in 1977. What did he say after the game?

He went mad! That was one of the funniest things I ever saw happen on a football field. I'd had a bit of a knock during the week leading up to the match, but I'd told Bill I was okay to play.

Then after we'd gone four-nil up he decided it was safe to give me a rest because we had another game in midweek. But he didn't know that a couple of the other lads had picked up knocks during the game. Mickey Allen had already told me that he was struggling so he said he'd go off instead. I ran over to Eddie Lyons who was holding the number above his head and told him to change it.

Then we heard a shout from Paul Walker to say that he was in a worse state than Mickey and that he should go off, so we told Eddie to change the number again. You were only allowed to make one substitution in those days remember.

Eddie Lyons had had enough by this stage, standing on the touch-line being messed around, I heard him shout "Oh fuck the lot of you!" then he threw all the numbers up in the air.

I once saw a great photo of Eddie walking away in a huff with all the numbers stuck in the mud. Bill had a right go at us, accusing the players of trying to make him look stupid in front of the crowd and the press, we had a laugh about it later though.

So you and Dodgin became really close?
We did, we saw a lot of each other away from the club too. He often used to ring me up in the evening, he'd ask, "everything all right at home?"... "Kids okay?".... "How about the missus?".... "Right then, get yourself in a taxi and meet me and Tommy Baldwin at the Richmond Wine Bar." And half an hour later I'd be sat down with Bill and 'The Old Sponge' sharing a bottle of red. Bill had originally asked me to be his player-coach but then decided to get Baldwin in, I didn't really mind at the time, he was another good drinking partner, I liked him.

As captain, Bill used to call me in to talk about the players and ask who I thought he should pick for certain matches, he also bought Pat Kruse on my say-so. [Laughs] Pat may be one ugly fucker but he was a brilliant footballer! Bill and I were talking about the need to buy a new defender and he asked me who I thought the best players were in our division, straight away I said "Pat Kruse".

Whenever we'd played against him we seemed to struggle getting past the bloke and he'd really impressed me. A week later Bill called me back in and said, "there you go Jackie, your mate Pat's in there, I've just signed him." I laughed, I'd never spoken to Pat, I didn't know him at all, but Bill was prepared to sign him because I thought he was a quality defender. He was another good drinker too, Pat didn't drink pints, he ate them!

Pat was a strong lad too, good in the air and a solid tackler, not to mention his arm wrestling skills! After we'd won promotion in 1978 all the players went away for a short break to celebrate and a little incident happened in a pub. The lads were all sitting around having a laugh when these two farmer's lads started glaring at us, and I heard one of them saying something about how soft footballers were. They were a bit drunk but really started giving us some shit because we were drinking Flaming Sambucas, "skinny, soft, girls" they were saying, they were big old lads too.

"We're not fucking sissies" Pat trumped up and marched over to this 'Popeye-like' farmer and offered him an arm wrestle. This bloke's arms were massive, but Pat knocked another pint back in one as we all gathered round their table. Pat then dropped to the floor and did twenty press-ups to get the blood pumping, sat back down, then Pat beat him! A massive cheer went up from the rest of the lads and the farmers had a good laugh with us for the rest of the afternoon. "Who's a skinny bastard now?" asked Pat!

Do you remember any other infamous drinking tales?
Oh there are hundreds, you could fill a whole book with them alone I would think! Another one that stands out involves Gordon Sweetzer. We became close after playing against each other in a training game while he was on trial at Brentford. We'd had a right go at each other on the pitch,

CULT BEES AND LEGENDS VOLUME TWO

Barry Tucker [far left], Stevie Phillips [centre] and Bill Dodgin at one of his numerous golf days

he was trying to give me grief, so I gave him one almighty elbow in the stomach which left him winded in a heap. When he eventually got up he chased me all over the pitch. The combination of his feisty attitude and what he was doing on the ball really impressed me.

After the game John Docherty asked me what I thought, my answer was simple, "sign him Doc, just sign him." Sweetzer was offered a contract soon after and he acknowledged I'd helped him out and we became pals. He was such a funny bloke, I'd never met anyone quite so lively. Sweetzer and Dodgin didn't see eye to eye though, the manager thought he was a nutter!

Anyway, all the players were at a Brentford FC Christmas Golf Day and I was sitting with Gordon at one of the sponsored tables when I was told, as club captain, I had to make a speech. I had to thank all and sundry for a great day etc., then wish everyone a happy Christmas on behalf of the club, blah, blah, blah. When I was told, Gordon immediately nudged me and told me he wanted to do it instead, I just laughed at the time, but when the time came to stand up, I felt him push my shoulder down while he stood up in my place.

He then set about taking the piss out of all the players, the manager, everyone... It was absolutely hilarious! Everywhere I looked there were players crying with laughter, we were wetting ourselves. Gordon later threw two glass ashtrays at a waiter for trying to close the bar, luckily that was after Dodgin had gone home. The next day I was called in to the manager's office to explain reports he'd heard that the Brentford captain had gone berserk... I had to explain that it wasn't the 'real' Brentford captain that had got a bit lively!

I can't imagine the Brentford players of today being allowed to get away with the kind of lifestyle that you were, can you?
Football has certainly changed for the better in that respect, don't get me wrong I loved every minute of my career, but I would probably have been a far better player if I'd had my time in the game now. But as much as we enjoyed ourselves, I never missed training and I'd always be up at the front pushing the lads harder.

I'd go out there on a Saturday and be prepared to die for the club, I lost count of the amount of confrontations myself and Gordon Sweetzer got involved in because we wanted to win for Brentford. Today's players may be more focused on their fitness and diet, but do you get the same commitment?

Looking back at your year-on-year appearance record at Brentford it struck me how remarkably consistent you were. Do you feel you were lucky to avoid major injuries during your playing career?

There were a few niggly injuries here and there, but you're right, nothing too serious. Although my knee gives me plenty of grief now and I may have to have a big operation soon.

I remember having trouble with my shoulder one season, which kept me out for a fair while, it was a viral infection rather than a football-related knock, but it had the medics baffled. I'd never experienced pain like it in my life, I was in agony for about two months, they gave me all sorts of pills and potions for it, but in the end I went to bed with a bottle of whisky and that seemed to do the trick... I had a bugger of a headache for two days but the shoulder was cured!

Eddie Lyons, the club physio, would deal with all the minor injuries though, what a wonderful man Eddie was. What a character. When I see modern day players huddled by the centre circle with their arms around each other before a kick-off, I always think of Eddie's pre-match huddles in the dressing room back in the 70s.

Eddie would make all the players form a circle before we came out on to the pitch and he'd start singing, "we're going to win-today, we're going to win-today", to the tune of 'Tararaboomdeay', while doing a little tap dance. Eddie also once made me gargle with strong disinfectant to clear up a sore throat I had, he didn't tell me it was industrial strength and it bleached the whole inside of my mouth and my lips white.

Have you kept many photos and press cuttings from your career?

I'm really not into all of that to be honest, I've got a few cuttings from when I was a kid but I was never one for tearing things out of the newspapers or asking for photographs. I'll probably regret it sooner or later though, I'm just about to become a grandfather for the first time so it would be good to be able to pass something on to them eventually. Not that I intend 'going' anywhere for a wee while yet!

After ten, long years your Brentford career came to a bit of an abrupt and unfortunate end. Bill Dodgin was axed in favour of Fred Callaghan. Was there a problem between you and the incoming manager?

I was never a lover of Fred, he was a good taxi driver, but that was about all. I had more respect for the players than he did, so I decided it was time for me to go. As soon as Fred got the job I had a rough idea what was going to happen so I started to make plans, but he never once had the balls to talk to me and tell me what he thought. Bill Dodgin should have been given more of a chance to get us out of relegation trouble before he was sacked, but Dan Tana obviously wasn't convinced we'd survive under Bill. Dodgin, Baldwin and myself had already agreed to up the training and up the fight, but time ran out before the changes could be made.

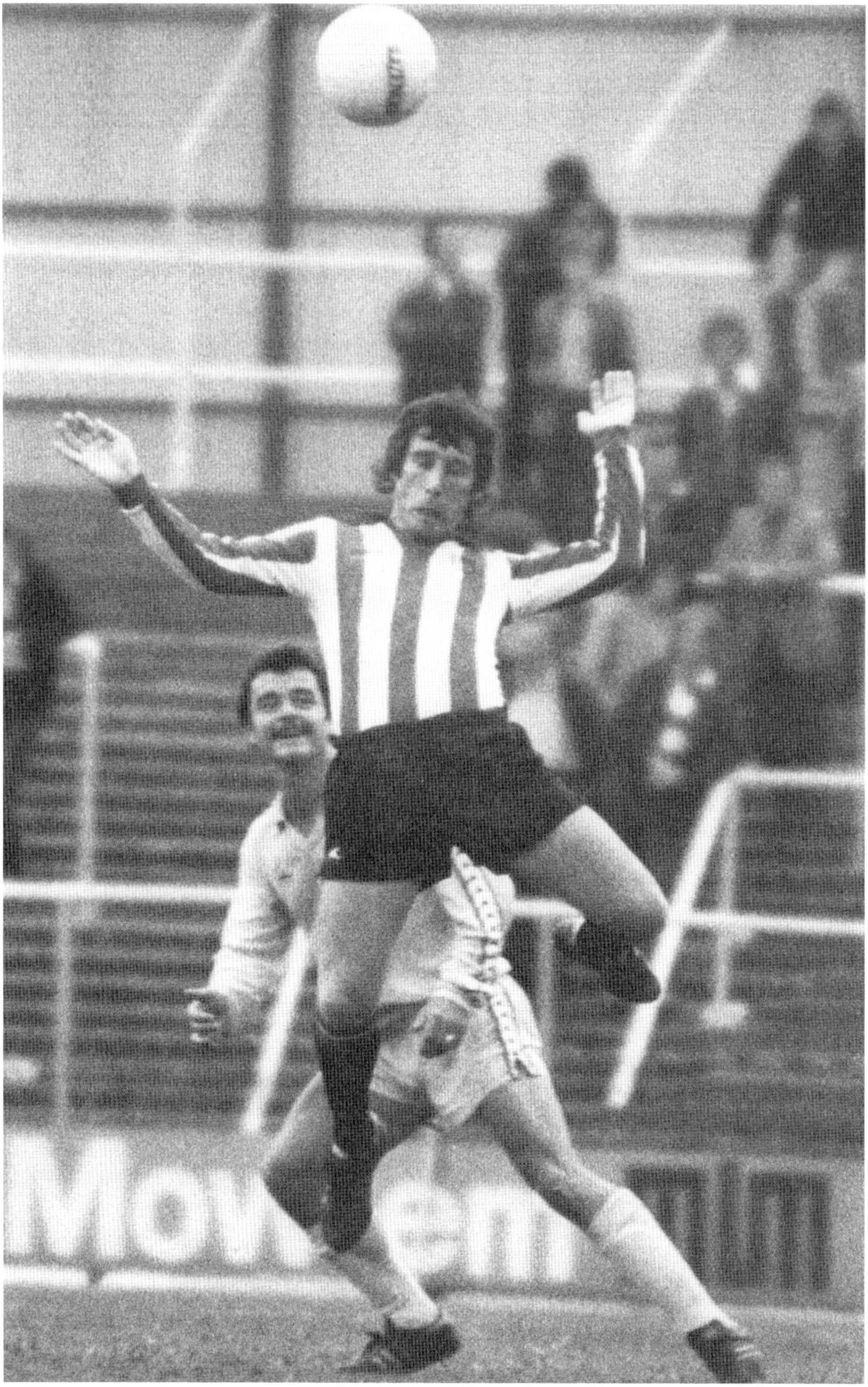
Mov

You went to play for Addlestone and Weybridge and were in the side that made the FA Cup First Round journey back to Griffin Park in 1981. Did you get a good reception?

I certainly did, it was one of those fairytale cup-ties that the FA Cup is so famous for, it was great for me anyway. Fred Callaghan and Ron Harris had been spying on us for a good few weeks leading up to the match so I made sure that we changed all our set piece routines and corners on the day. I told the other players that if we were lucky enough to get anywhere near the Brentford goal we had to swap things around.

After going two-nil up Brentford took their foot off the gas a bit and it allowed us to get back into the match. We scored a couple of late goals, changing the routines worked because the equaliser was something we tried for the first time, all the Brentford defenders were marking the near post because that's what they had been told to do. [Laughs] Fred went mad at the Bees players after the game I heard.

Looking back, how would you describe yourself as a player?

That's a really hard thing for me to answer. I certainly would never let anyone down, I could be an aggressive player at times, I could tackle, run and had two good feet I thought. I would say I was alright.

After ten years service did you feel you were treated shoddily?

Probably at the time I did, aye, but I don't hold grudges to be honest. I had a testimonial match against Watford at Griffin Park a couple of years after I had left which was a good night.

How did you cope with life in the 'big wide world' after football?

Oh I hated it, I really struggled to cope to be honest. I had to though, I had two small kids to support, but doing 'real' work was awful, I'm no worker. A Brentford fan who I'd got to know really well offered me a job in an engineer's works, but I just wouldn't adapt, my heart just wasn't in it.

That was a sad day when I turned up and had to sit behind an oil-stinking lathe instead of running about a training ground with the lads. Nothing can ever prepare you for that stomach-wrenching feeling. I run a cleaning contractor's business now though, which gives me a bit more independence at least.

How do you look back at your time at Brentford?

With a great deal of affection. I made some great friends at the club, friends I've remained close to after all these years, and the two promotion seasons I enjoyed at the club were truly special. We played some good stuff for the fans, and although there were a few moments when things weren't so good, they were happy days. Very happy days.

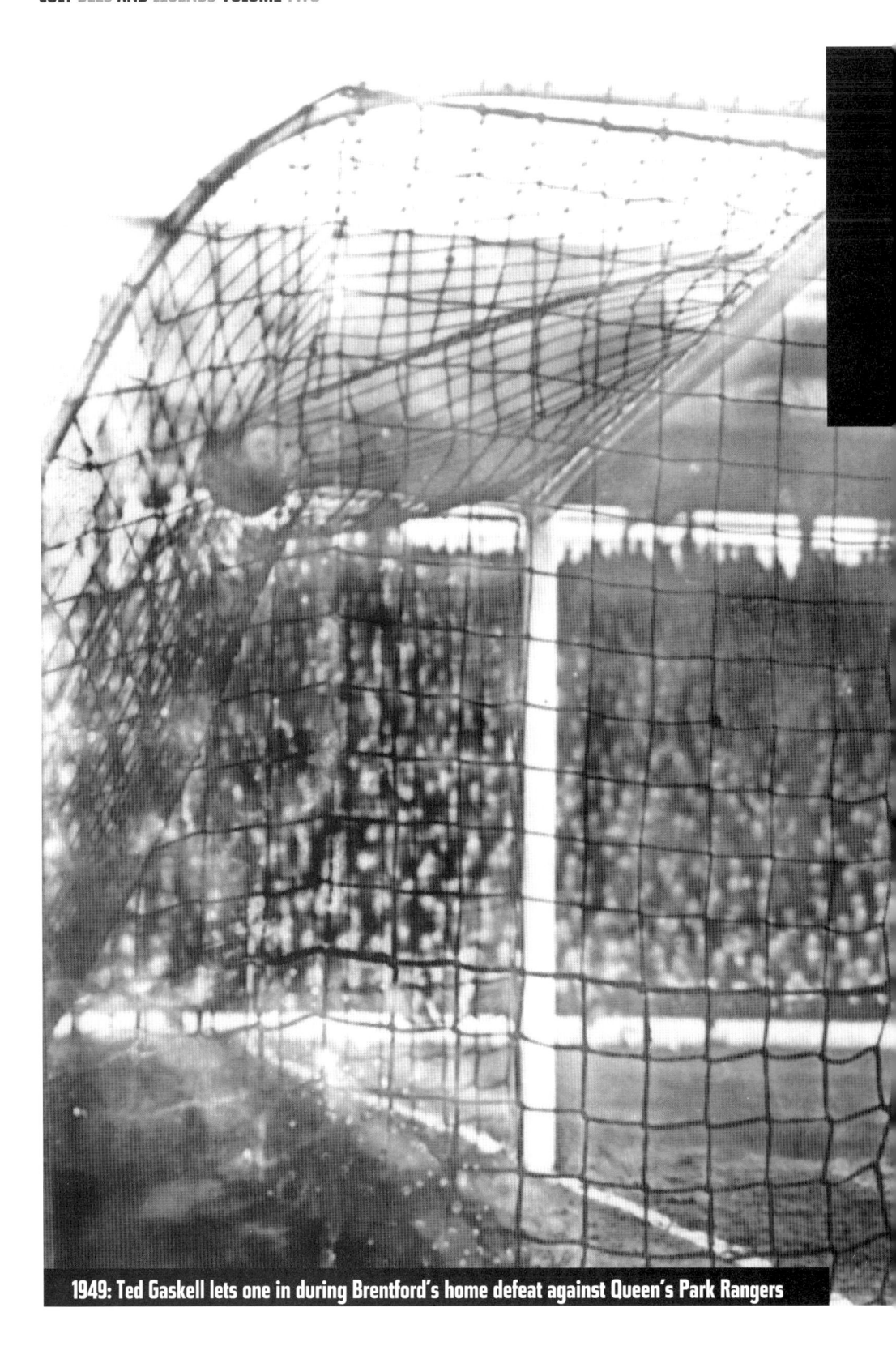

1949: Ted Gaskell lets one in during Brentford's home defeat against Queen's Park Rangers

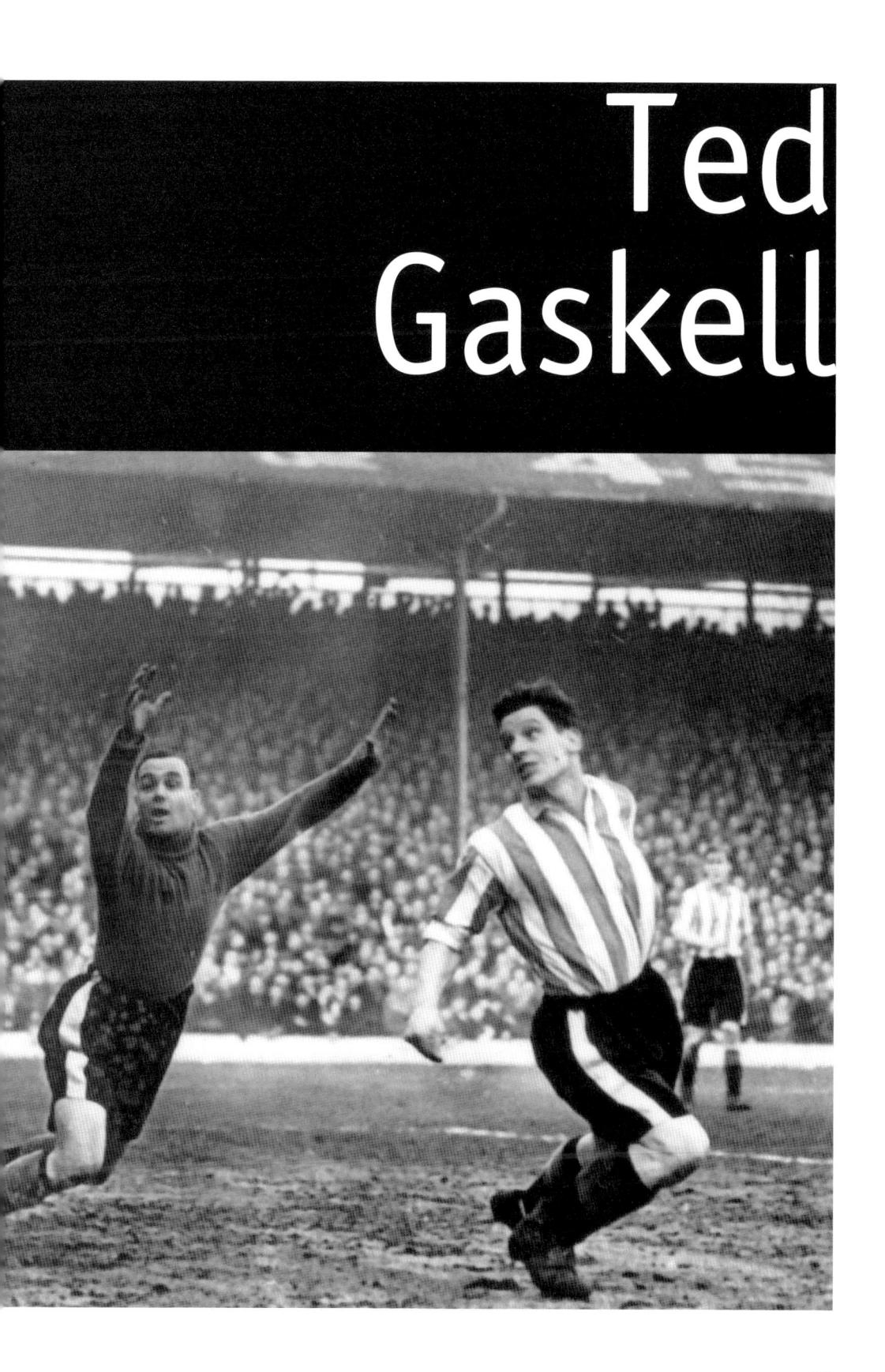

Ted Gaskell

Holding the club record as Brentford's oldest surviving player is a precarious honour, but Ted Gaskell is a healthy and happy chap who will hopefully hold on to the title for many years to come. Longevity aside, Ted holds a more unusual club record, signed in 1937 by the great Harry Curtis, the Cheshire born goalie didn't make his Brentford first team debut for more than ten years.

Obviously the distractions caused by a certain Adolf Hitler played a big part in that statistic, but none-the-less it still seems an amazing amount of time to wait for your first game at a new club. In fact Gaskell's first team opportunities were limited to just thirty-eight games between 1936 and 1952, but that shouldn't disguise the fact that he became one of the club's longest serving players.

Like many players of Ted's generation, World War Two robbed them of their prime footballing years, not to mention close friends and family in many cases, so when hostilities ended in 1945, Gaskell faced an uncertain future at Griffin Park. So it was a big relief to the 'keeper that despite a plethora of goalies guesting for The Bees while Ted was away on National Service, he was kept on after the War where he continued to train with the finest set of players ever to wear the club's colours.

Ted Gaskell, who now lives with his daughter in Berkshire, is one of the few remaining links with Brentford's halcyon, First Division days and I hope you agree his memories are priceless.

Ted, your accent suggests you weren't born and bred in West London, where did your footballing story begin?

I was born in the Peak District and as a boy played for several local sides, including Romiley St. Chads and Stockport County, before moving to Chesterfield in 1936.

At the end of my first season they decided not to retain me, in fact the six-week period after leaving Saltergate was the only time I was ever out of work. I then decided to write to all the clubs in the Cheshire League to see if I could get a new club, then Buxton contacted me to say they were looking for a goalie and would I come along for a trial.

A little while after joining I was asked to play in the annual Cheshire League versus Southern League match up there, which attracted a lot of scouts from League clubs. They would come along to look for promising new players, and it was at that fixture in 1937 when Buxton's captain, Sid Tuffnel, put a good word in for me and tipped off one of the scouts about my ability.

The bloke had come to watch a lad by the name of Bailey, who was playing for Stalybridge Celtic, but Sid told him that Aston Villa and Manchester United had been sniffing round me and he should get in quick. Anyway, the scout passed my name on to Brentford and things progressed from there.

So Manchester United were watching you, did they talk to you about a move to Old Trafford?

I was asked to travel to Manchester for a trial but I said "no, I don't think so!" The fact that I was a big Manchester City fan didn't really come into it, but financially I was doing very nicely at Buxton, combining football and another job, digging holes for the council. Buxton were playing twice a week and were paying some expenses too, so I was doing alright I thought, I knew I was better off where I was than by becoming a full-time pro with United.

Perhaps you should write to Manchester United now and say you've changed your mind?

[Laughs] It's a different world for a footballer in this day and age, it really is.

So what made you move to Brentford rather than United?

Well, Brentford paid £500 for me, that was a big fee for Buxton and a record for a local lad. For the first month after I arrived at Griffin Park, The Bees were top of the First Division. Brentford were the top side then. I remember travelling down to the club on a Friday night to sign my contract the next morning and I was met by Jimmy Bain at the station and taken to my new digs in Windmill Road. Originally I was supposed to be sharing a room with Arthur Bateman, our full-back from the First Division side, because he had been commuting every day from Southend. But in the end I shared with a player called Ted Farrelly who came down from Scotland for a couple of seasons before being transferred to Northampton.

What players impressed you when you arrived?

Oh they were all very good, Duncan McKenzie, Joe James, Dai Hopkins, plus the trio from Brentford's feeder club Middlesbrough - Billy Scott, Jack Holliday and Ernie Muttit. Dai Hopkins and Bobby Reid were very special I thought, but in the reserves The Bees had another two wingers who were also capable of taking on anyone, George Wilkins and Leslie Smith. They were good enough to walk into the first team of virtually any other club in the land. Harry Curtis had assembled a very impressive side.

What was Harry Curtis like as a man?

Because he hadn't played the game at the highest level I wouldn't describe Harry as a player's manager, but as far as team-building and handling a crowd of blokes was concerned, he was very good. Consequently Brentford was a really happy club.

Joe James and George Poyser were always going in to Harry's office asking if they could finish training early so they could go and take in a football match at Arsenal or somewhere… Harry used to say, "Oh not you two again, what time do you want to knock off today?" To his credit Harry would normally agree, but instead of being just the one or two who were allowed to go, the manager would telephone ahead and get tickets for everyone, even the backroom staff. We would all go together. That was typical of Harry, he would include everyone. The Guvnor's battle cry before games was always the same, I remember him telling the players, "Get stuck in and bang it up the middle!"

I got very friendly with Harry and his family, I was a single bloke at the time and got to know his two sons, Gordon and Ron, very well. He used to live in a big house called Doring Court, opposite Swyncombe Avenue that runs up from South Ealing, it was a lovely house with a big garden and a billiards room. When Harry was at home he was just a normal bloke, you wouldn't have thought he was one of the top football managers in the land, Harry Curtis was a very good man.

Dai Hopkins is another of those iconic names from that era, how would you describe him?
He was a very good player, but a bit 'Welsh' if you know what I mean! [Laughs] He was a bit 'sharp' and quick to take offence at times, he never found it easy to work out if he was having his leg pulled or not. A wonderful footballer though.

What was the goalkeeping situation at Brentford when you arrived?
Joe Crozier had been brought in from East Fife a year before I arrived. Harry Curtis wanted Joe to take over from Jimmy Mathieson who was at the end of his career. I was only twenty and was signed to be Crozier's understudy. It was unusual for lads as young as me to get into the first team in those days, clubs preferred more experienced players and seemed to nurse the lads for longer. Crozier was a very good goalie in my eyes, a brilliant shot-stopper.

I was a bit unlucky when I first arrived at Brentford really, I picked up a knee injury playing for the reserves in the London Combination which meant I had to go into hospital in the summer of 1938 to have an operation. Because of the injury and the time I was out, Brentford bought another goalie, Frank Clack, from Birmingham City. Then just as I was starting to make my recovery, War broke out and all football players had their contracts terminated.

Did you spend a lot of time training with Joe Crozier?
Well, we kicked the ball about a bit with each other, but there were no special goalkeeping routines like there are now.

The War must have been a very unsettling time, not least because the country was at arms with Germany, but what happened to you and the other players?

I will always remember all the Brentford squad and club staff crowded into Harry Curtis' office listening to Prime Minister, Neville Chamberlain, telling the nation that we were at war with Germany. There was a dark mood in the office afterwards as we all talked about what had been said and what we all thought would happen, then all of a sudden we heard an air raid siren go off!

It turned out to be a false alarm, but the shocked look on the players' faces was a picture, we were thinking 'surely it can't start that quickly', but we'd seen the newsreels of Germany bombing Poland, so it could have been possible.

The Football League was suspended after a handful of games of the 1939-40 season. Some players decided to go back to their home towns to be with their families before joining the forces, while others decided to stay in and around Brentford because they had joined the police war reserves.

Football soon made a come-back and regional divisions were set up. It was fairly common practice for the police to fiddle around with their player's shift rostas so the footballers would be available to play for Brentford, they'd put the players on nights in the early part of the week and make sure they were available to play at the weekend.

Looking at the attendance figures for the time, football fans were staying away in big numbers. Obviously there were more pressing matters to consider during wartime?

You're right, but the ground capacities had been reduced by over half for safety reasons, which exaggerated things. I remember playing at Arsenal in the early days of the War and there was hardly anyone there, but their striker Ted Drake was still going in for the ball as if he was playing in front of a full house. Ted was a strong player who used to go in hard. As I watched him chase down one through-ball I just knew that if I went down to pick the ball up he wasn't going to stop or back out and that he was about to clatter into me. As he lunged for the ball I remained upright, straightened my leg and put my boot and studs right behind the ball to block him... Ted went flying!

George Poyser shouted over to me, "are you trying to kill yourself for thirty shillings Ted?" Then Drake came over and threatened to throw me over the barriers and on to the terracing, so Poyser lumped him one! There was a bit of rough stuff dished out from time to time, but certainly none of those sickening over the ball 'tackles'.

So George Poyser could look after himself as well as his team-mates?

George learned his trade with Port Vale and was a cracking full-back. I remember one game against Stoke we came up against Stanley Matthews, who was top of the shop at the time.

George knew Stan from his time in the town, and when they shook hands before the game kicked off I heard him say to Matthews, "right, if you get

1937: A copy of a colour portrait of Ted Gaskell shortly after arriving at Brentford

the ball in front of me Stanley you just whip it over rather than trying to run round me. Then we shall both be happy. If you start any of that fancy business I promise I will chase you all over the pitch kicking you!" They both laughed and carried on chatting.

I take it you joined the Forces when the hostilities started?
Yes I was stationed down at Aldershot and trained to be an Army Physical Training Instructor. Harry Curtis told me that it was inevitable that I would be called up so I may as well line myself up with a regiment and a role that I would enjoy. So he had a word with Maurice Edelston, an amateur England international playing for Brentford, who by that stage had got a job in the Army too. Edleston was trying to gather men from all sports together; football, cricket, boxing, the lot, so I went along too and ended up staying there for the whole war.

Frank Swift, the great Manchester City goalkeeper was in there too, we were great friends, as well as stars like Dennis Compton, Bill Shankly and Matt Busby, whose bunk was opposite mine. Matt Busby and myself were both Catholics and we used to go to church together on Sundays. In fact Busby played a game for Brentford during the War.

I managed to play a few games for Brentford before I went down to Aldershot full-time though, in the newly formed Regional League and Subsidiary Competition. But after I went into barracks I was told that Saturdays would be a busy time for me and I couldn't carry on turning out for The Bees.

Consequently my next game for Brentford wasn't until almost the end of the War. A lot of goalies guested for the club in that time, including Johnny Jackson and Wrexham's Welsh international, George Poland.

You were fortunate enough to have played with some of the greatest names in Brentford's history, who were the best in your mind?
It's difficult to say really, there were just so many good players at the club during that era, I'm not sure it's right to pick individuals out as being better than the others after all this time. But if you forced me to pick out the greatest player while I was at Brentford I would say Jim Towers. He really set the place alight, ask any fan who has been going for a number of years and they'll tell you what a fantastic football player Jim was, and what a nice man too.

There was another player who was emerging at the club when I was leaving who I thought was truly special, Peter Gelson. He was a cracking centre-half, in a class of his own at Brentford. With the right grooming Gelson could have played for England I think. As a young lad I could see his potential and I used to urge Malcolm McDonald, who'd progressed to manager by that stage, to give him a run in the reserves. But for some reason McDonald and Jackie Goodwin, who was coaching the young lads, thought it would be more beneficial for the club to have the best possible youth side.

If Gelson had been tested out against a more mature and experienced opposition earlier I think he would have gone all the way in the game. I felt a lot of the good, young prospects from that era were held back to some extent.

Do you remember anything about the War League game with Queen's Park Rangers at Griffin Park in December 1939? The score remained nil-nil with sixty-five minutes played, but The Bees managed to lose seven-nil with you in goal?

Fortunately not! You'll find that goalies tend to try and forget the games when they let in lots of goals. I won't argue with the records, but we played all sorts of games around that time, they were little more than friendlies really, especially with so many guest players turning out.

Could you have played for Aldershot as a guest goalkeeper?

[Laughs] Aldershot probably had the best team in the world during the War! Their manager used to stand outside our gymnasium and basically pick a side made up of full internationals, some of the players had a list of caps as long as your arm.

Brentford struggled after the War and when the Football League was started again in 1946 The Bees were relegated from the top flight. Harry Curtis stepped aside too, it really was an end of a great era for the club. How do you remember that time?

Well I think it was a case that the club's best players before The War had obviously aged and some were past their best, including myself. I was twenty when I signed and by the time I started playing again, I was twenty-eight. I'd missed my prime years as a player and a lot of experience. Some of the players were over forty by the time they returned from the forces.

Harry Curtis had spent a lot of money on the team just before war had broken out only to see the players' contracts cancelled, so I think the club were quite hard up. But there were a lot of good players floating around trying to fix themselves up with clubs.

I remember hearing Tom Manley, who had signed for Brentford from Manchester United, telling Harry Curtis and Billy Lane, one of the scouts for Brentford who had played for the club in the late Twenties, that he'd served with a great player in the Middle East. He went on to say that he wasn't fixed up with a club and told the duo that the player had been on Middlesbrough's books, but had expressed an interest in joining Brentford. The player's name was Wilf Mannion.

Harry sent somebody to take a look at the player but the scout didn't recommend him for some reason. Mannion went on to play more than twenty-five games for England and became one of the star names from that era.

It must have been a sad day for you when Harry Curtis left?

It was, yes, it seemed he'd been manoeuvred out rather than Harry wanting to go. I remember going up to the manager's office one day to ask him something, only to see the director, Frank Davis, at his desk. I asked Davis, "have you seen The Guvnor?", only to be told, "I am The Guvnor!" I thought, "aye, aye, the old order has changed here..." The two Davis brothers, Frank and Harry were the top men at the club then, Frank had a pub up in Hanwell and Harry had a builders and decorators business. Then Jackie Gibbons became manager.

But there were a lot of changes around that time, Joe Crozier retired and I became the first choice goalie for a while. I was in the side for the start of the 1949-50 season when we had Tottenham at Griffin Park on the opening day.

We had a young side by then and lost four-one, but they printed in The People newspaper the next day that if it hadn't been for me, Spurs would have won by an even bigger margin. Bill Nicholson was the right-half that day, they had a great side and won the league that year.

I know the War was to blame, but it still seems a remarkable fact that you had to wait over ten years before making your league debut!

Yes I know, I think you'll find it was almost eleven years in fact, but you're right, the War played a big part in that.

The Spurs match was the first game that I was recognised as the number one goalie, and there was something else significant about that game, Ken Coote made his Brentford debut that day. After that Ken went on and on and is still the record appearance holder for the club.

Poor old Ken is dead now, but I vividly remember his club house in Whitton, and Brentford defender Tony Harper used to live next door. When Tony first arrived at Brentford he lived with my wife and me for a while.

Tony Harper's name doesn't crop up very often, what was he like?

Before he moved in with us he used to travel back to his home in Oxford every day, but he always used to struggle after a match. We lost count of the times he would come in to training on a Monday morning and say that he'd fallen asleep on the Paddington to Oxford train, only to be woken up in Birmingham. In the end he just had to live closer, so he moved in with me for a while. I remember my wife always hiding his fags!

So did you have your ten-year testimonial match before you'd even played for The Bees?

Not a match, no, but I was given a benefit cheque for £750 in 1948. All League players were given a similar payment after ten years service, but we had to pay tax on that, so in the end I only got around £450. I had a testimonial match in 1953 against my friends at other London football clubs.

It seems obscene that these days, at a time when players earn so much more than in your era, that they don't have to pay tax on their testimonials or benefit payments.
The clubs had players over a barrel too, if they decided not to retain a player at the end of the season, the player wasn't allowed to find a new club straight away as a free agent. They were still tied to their club for a few months in case the manager changed his mind, or they got a transfer fee for the player. If you couldn't find a new club it meant a summer without wages. It was a situation that eventually led to Jimmy Hill helping to scrap the maximum wage and fight for a better deal for the players.

Looking at the fixture lists, Christmas Day and Boxing Day matches were a common occurrence. Two matches over the holiday period must have ruined your home celebrations as players?
Absolutely, but depending on how the calendar fell at Christmas, players would sometimes have three games in four days; Christmas Day, Boxing Day, then another on the Saturday. It was stupidity really, Christmas Day fixtures would kick-off around mid-day, so if we were away we'd have to travel down the night before, Christmas Eve. Then after the match, we had to get back to London with the opposition team on the same train. That's the way they arranged the fixtures then, whoever we played on Christmas Day would be the opposition the next day, and they weren't always local sides either. Hull, Oldham, Sheffield United, Leicester... They were all Christmas opponents around that time.

So after injury and Hitler's distractions, the start of the 1949-50 season saw your first real run in the side?
Yes I played the first fourteen games that season until I got injured again up at Elland Road, Leeds at the end of October. I remember going in for a ball with Frank Dudley, who later played for Brentford, and I got a kick in the kidney. I had to play on and we lost one-nil, but I was in a lot of pain.
The manager, Jackie Gibbons, asked me if I was able to travel home with the team because he didn't want to leave me in a hospital up there. Anyway, I got the train back to London, then the club coach back to the club, where they arranged a taxi to get me home. But the next morning I was passing blood, so I went down to the ground and told them, before being whipped in to Brentford Cottage Hospital.
On the Monday night the director and surgeon, Dr. Radley-Smith, came in to visit me and told the doctors that if I wasn't feeling better the next morning, he would have to consider an operation. On the one hand I was lucky because I did feel better and was told to rest for a few weeks, but on the other I lost my place in the side to Alf Jefferies, and because he was playing so well, didn't get my place back until just after the beginning of the next season.

The War years, Ted Gaskell [middle row, third from right] and his Army football team

Ted Gaskell [back row fourth from left] and the post-War Brentford squad

But you only played a couple of matches during the 1950-51 season?

Well I played away at Preston and at home to Coventry, and although we lost both games I was happy with my performances. The next Saturday Brentford were playing at Maine Road, Manchester City, the club I'd supported as a lad. I thought 'brilliant!' I'd sorted out tickets for all my family and friends to come along to watch the game, I was really looking forward to the match.

All the newspapers had printed a team with my name on it in midweek, but when the manager's sheet went up on the Friday, Alf Jefferies' name filled the number one space. That really upset me as I would have loved nothing more than to have played against City while I was a professional.

I had another extended run the next season, the year we had a good FA Cup run. We knocked Queen's Park Rangers out three-one at Griffin Park in front of over 35,000 fans, before being taken to three games by Luton Town in Round Four. We drew the first game two-all after being two goals down at Luton, then in the replay, on the day King George VI died, we drew again nil-nil. I still remember Billy Dare making a great run, going through Luton like a dose of salts, rounding their goalkeeper, only to put the ball wide.

In those days, after a game at each venue, a second replay had to be played at a neutral ground, and because Arsenal was halfway between Brentford and Luton, Highbury Stadium was used. Jimmy Hill got a bad attack of cramp near the end of that game, and while we were messing about trying to get him sorted out, Luton scored the winner.

They went through three-two in front of almost 40,000 people, but it should have been Brentford playing Portsmouth in the Quarter-Final. I only played one more game for Brentford after that, Reg Newton was given the nod ahead of me then.

So I went in to see Jackie Gibbons to ask why I'd been dropped and to tell him that I'd had enough, that I was going to retire at the end of the season. He tried to talk me out of it, but I'd made my mind up. I told him that I didn't feel there was any point hanging around Griffin Park for any longer and that I didn't fancy a transfer to another club because my family was settled in the area. I said that as far as I was concerned I might as well hang my gloves up. I remember Harold Palmer writing a nice piece about me in The Standard when the news came out.

Jackie Gibbons' reign as manager didn't carry on for much longer either, but I guess the board were in awe of their new signing Tommy Lawton and thought he was the man to take Brentford to the top flight again.

Tommy Lawton was a massive signing for the club, although I'm sure he only came to Griffin Park for the money. He'd been around the clubs a bit before arriving at Brentford... As a lad he was at Burnley, then after the War he signed for Everton.

He didn't settle in Liverpool too long, then he moved down to Chelsea, then on to Notts County, then Brentford. But he was a real crowd-puller, wherever he played supporters would turn out, he was a great player, but as a manager... Oh dear! Tommy used to drive around in a big AC car, so he already had a few bob!

Before Lawton was promoted to manager Jackie Gibbons seemed to be struggling and it was rumoured that his player-coach, Malcolm McDonald [later to become manager himself], was picking the team. Malcolm was a lovely man too and was godfather to my daughter Claire, and Johnny Pointon was the same to my daughter Julia.

It sounds as if you were very close to your team-mates?
Yes, I was good friends with our defender George Paterson too, what a smart man he was. He used to buy all his clothes from Dunns up in London, he was always immaculately turned out. He wasn't objectionable with it, George just took pride in his appearance.

Do you remember anything of your trip up to Scotland in 1950 when Brentford were invited to take on Celtic?
I do yes, Malcolm McDonald, who'd played at Celtic for years before coming to Brentford had helped set the friendly up, but that was some journey!

We'd played Plymouth on the Saturday before, so we'd travelled down to the West Country on Friday, then after the match, we travelled back over night, went home to get changed and get some more clothes, then caught another overnight train up to Scotland on Sunday. We played Celtic on the Monday night, drew two-all, then we had to get home again!

Do you remember your other high profile trips with Brentford?
We travelled out to Amsterdam with Brentford to play against the Dutch national side and drew one-all. I remember going out to Sweden too, where Dai Hopkins had moved to and was coaching a side by the name of Sliepner. Brentford played very well on that tour, drawing the first game nil-all, then winning the rest of the four games. Unfortunately the England side, who were over there for an international match in Stockholm at the same time, didn't do quite as well.

We all got tickets to go and watch the international but England got beaten by the Swedes three-one, they had two inside-forwards playing for them at the time, Garvis Carlsson and Gunnar Gren, 'cor, they were shit-hot. Sweden also had a big centre-forward, Hans Jeppson, who played for Charlton Athletic, it was like stopping a battle ship when those three got going. I remember the talk among the newspaper chaps after the match was that the selectors should have picked the eleven men from Brentford!

August 1949: Ted Gaskell foils Tottenham's Eddie Baily at Griffin Park

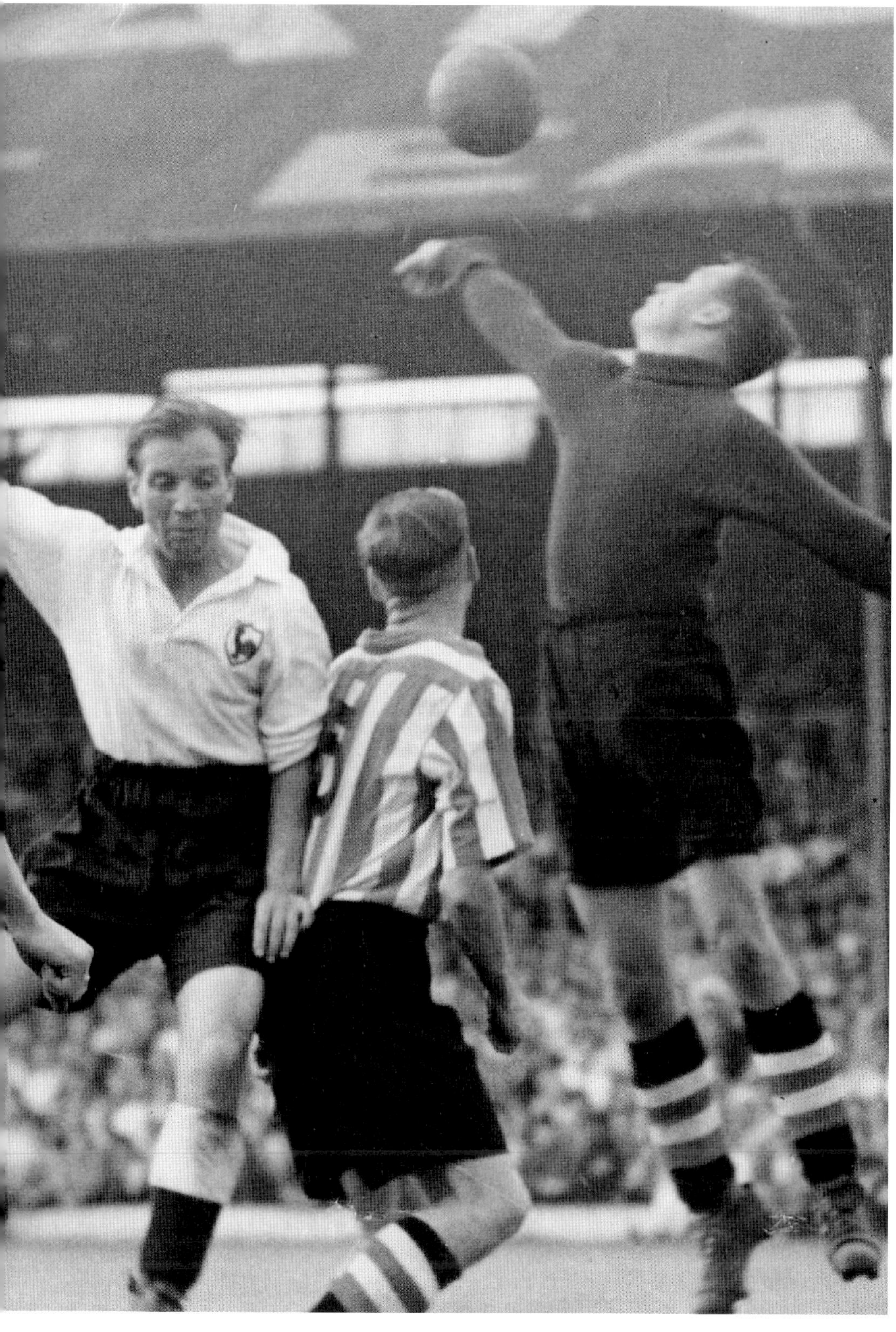

It was a difficult era to be a goalie, the rules offered you precious little protection, your clothing was ridiculous and the pitches were atrocious... How did you cope?
[Laughs] Griffin Park was our training ground too, so you can imagine what a state the pitch was in during the winter months, we used to play on mud baths. They used to put sharp sand all over the penalty area sometimes, but that used to cut you to ribbons when you dived. I even remember walking around my area before a game picking out bits of glass from the gravel.

You'd just about be getting a scab forming on your elbow or knees then you'd knock it off again, I was covered in small scars. I used to wear a woollen roll-neck jersey, a cap and thin wool gloves, not those great padded things they've got today!

As you were the nearest man to the supporters behind the goal most of the time, do you recall much banter with the crowd back then?
There was always a good rapport with the fans, apart from when you went to Millwall. They were as bad then as they are now. When you came out on the pitch at The Den it seemed as if you had to walk through the crowd, they were so close. I remember them throwing stones, or whatever they could lay their hands on, at us. Eventually the club were forced to put fencing up to protect the players as they ran out, which stopped the visiting team being hit with objects, but the fans would spit at you instead.

I remember playing for the reserves there in 1939 and we were having a terrible time, we were really under pressure and Millwall had done everything except score. Then, with about five minutes to go, Brentford got a penalty, which Len Townsend thumped in. A few minutes later, as we were defending a corner, Tom Manley, who was the Brentford full-back that day, was guarding the near post. The fans behind the goal were giving him some stick about the penalty, so he turned round and said, "that'll stop you farting in church!" I'm not sure what he meant by it, but I had a few words with Tom because the crowd were hurling abuse and all sorts, and I had to stand there and take it as the play moved away from my penalty area.

I remember Leyton Orient were a bit rough and going there was a bit dicey sometimes, as was West Ham. I think there must be something in the air over in the East End! But over all I used to love travelling to away games, going up on the train on a Friday and stopping in a nice hotel with all the players, they were happy days.

It must have been terrible for the Brentford players a few years later when the club went through some hard times and all the players were taking their kit home to wash themselves and travelling up to long distance away games on the match day to save money. I used to feel sorry for players like Ken Coote, lads who had sampled the good life, then had to adapt to the hardship.

Did you have a favourite away ground?

I used to really enjoy playing at Fratton Park, Portsmouth. At the time there were big Navy barracks down there and more often than not, even for a reserve fixture, there'd be a decent crowd in. There'd be a fair few Brentford fans down there too.

What's your most vivid memory of Griffin Park itself?

The huge stand behind the Brook Road goal. As a goalie it was tremendous to stand right in front of it when that stand was full to the rafters. At one stage I think they were considering making it even bigger and adding another tier. There were also plans to buy up all the houses along New Road and extend on that side too, but the War put a stop to all of that. The War changed a lot of things at Brentford.

What a tragedy to have pulled the Brook Road stand down, it really was. I know a lot of people who stopped going the day that stand came down.

What did you do after football Ted?

I got involved with coaching the Brentford A team for a while as well as working at Platt's Grocers in Hounslow. They had about thirty shops all over the Hounslow area, but they eventually sold out to Mac Fisheries. I also did a lot of coaching with George Smith, a big centre-half who played for Brentford for a few games at the end of the 1946-47 season. He asked me if I'd like to get involved with training and coaching the England side at Bisham Abbey before international matches, and I jumped at the chance. Walter Winterbottom was the England coach then, but there was a selection committee who used to pick the side at the time.

Walter set up a coaching programme which used to travel around to the schools and help with the boys, I was involved with coaching for the London FA too. At one stage there was talk about me going over to Australia to help set up their new Football Association's coaching programme, but for one reason or another that didn't happen.

I then went to work for Customs where I managed to get twenty years under my belt and a decent pension.

Jim Towers

February 1961: Jim Towers scores one of two goals against Chesterfield at Griffin Park

Whenever I hear the name Jim Towers mentioned I think of two things; firstly George Francis' name immediately springs to mind, Jim's life-long strike partner, and secondly, goals. Lots of them. Jim's scoring record is truly awesome, in 262 league appearances Towers netted 153 times and he scored at that rate pretty much everywhere he played in a fabulous career in front of goal.

Quite why Jim Towers never took the opportunity to prove himself in the top flight God only knows, because of his modern day contemporaries, very few can boast a similar ratio of goals to games. But as Jim explains in his interview, the maximum wage restrictions meant that players of his generation had a very different outlook on the draw of top flight football, and about life in general. In this day and age, with multi-million pound wage packets and the super-star lifestyles that top strikers enjoy, it is sometimes difficult to comprehend quite how contrasting players aspirations were.

One thing remains constant though; selling your best players to your deadliest local rivals is as unpopular amongst a club's loyal fan base today as it ever was. So imagine the rage of the Griffin Park faithful during the summer of 1961 when both Jim Towers and George Francis, scorers of a combined eighty-seven goals in the previous two seasons, were packed off to Queen's Park Rangers for a derisory joint fee of £8,000. Was that the day that the balance of power shifted in West London football forever?

Anyway, the loss of the Terrible Twins' goals left Brentford virtually impotent up front, and it wasn't long before the Board regretted their decision massively, so much so that they went back to Rangers and tried to buy Towers back. A fee was agreed and QPR looked to make a handsome profit.

Unfortunately somebody threw a massive spanner in the works, a catastrophic breakdown in communications by Bees manager Malcolm McDonald put an end to the deal. Instead of meeting his Rangers counterpart at Brentford Market, as agreed, the Bee's boss turned up at Acton Market, and alas, the window of opportunity had gone forever. QPR changed their minds after being stood up and Brentford were relegated at the end of the season. If only mobile phones were around forty years earlier!

Although Jim Towers didn't get the chance to make a return and continue where he'd left off, his achievements will be remembered at the club for all time. Towers is undoubtedly one of the finest, if not the finest, forwards to have ever pulled on the red and white stripes of Brentford.

Did you have any trials with other London clubs before Brentford picked you up?

I'd been down to Fulham for a try-out, they were the team I supported as a kid, and I used to go to Craven Cottage with my family right up until I signed as a professional. There were dozens of kids being put through their paces that day, we were given a bib and took it in turns to get about five minutes each in a game with rolling substitutes, which was a stupid way to judge lads.

So many good players must have slipped through the net, if you weren't lucky enough to get the ball or do something with it while you were on the pitch then you didn't get asked back.

There was a bloke wandering around the pitch touching kids on the head saying, "you won't make it, you can stay, you can go..." I'll always remember that. Shortly afterwards I joined Brentford juniors.

What are your early memories at the club when you joined in 1948?

I wouldn't exactly call the set-up very organised, it was pretty run-of-the-mill to be honest, but Alf Bute ran the juniors and made the decision to sign up kids. He had the pick of all the local talent and there were several school-boy internationals on the books.

We played all kinds of teams all over the borough, I must have played on every pitch in the area, and we would beat everyone, which was a complete waste of time because the games weren't competitive enough. Eventually things got better though and we started playing against the juniors from other professional clubs.

I was fairly lucky to get my chance at Brentford really, at the age of eighteen, just before I went in to the Army to do my National Service in 1951, I was offered a professional contract. At the time their decision seemed a bit of a lottery, pot-luck almost. Then when I was de-mobbed two years later Tommy Lawton was manager and Brentford had fifty-seven professionals on their books and three teams. I'd missed two years of football which meant it was difficult to catch up.

I'd played a bit in the forces and done quite well, representing the regiment and battalion side, then the British Army of the Rhine team, but it wasn't the same as being at Brentford and my game suffered. I felt I'd fallen behind everyone else. My saving grace was that I was always able to get a goal from somewhere, which gets you noticed. Bit by bit I adjusted to the faster pace and got into the reserves, then I started scoring a lot of goals.

What also must have helped you break through was Bill Dodgin senior's policy of youth?

Yeah, under Tommy Lawton he picked a lot of the older players, people like Frankie Broome, and he had a very experienced squad to pick from. In fact I remember playing in a friendly at Hayes under Lawton and there were four international players that turned out for Brentford. But Dodgin was building for the future and gave a lot of the youngsters who I'd come through the ranks with a chance to prove themselves in the first team, players like Dennis Heath and of course myself.

Whenever your name is mentioned, George Francis' is normally used in the same breath. Your paths had continually crossed, when was the first time you met your future striking partner?

The first time I met George was when our Saturday morning cinema teams played against each other. I played for the Gaumont in Shepherd's Bush, George's side were from the Odeon in Acton.

After that we were both in the same Irish Fusiliers regiment in the Army, we were stationed in Germany at similar times, and although I was slightly older and came back to Brentford ahead of him, we linked up again there. It was all pure coincidence.

Did you ever feel there was any competition between the pair of you to score the most goals?

Not really, as long as we were both fit we both played, and between 1956 and 1961 we only missed a handful of games between us. George was a different kind of player to me anyway, he was very quick around the box, he chased the ball down and forced defenders to make mistakes and because of that he scored a lot more goals than me inside the area.

He was a real nuisance, whereas I wasn't like that at all. He made a lot of goals for himself, where I would wait for the right pass or cross, and I scored with a lot of shots from outside the box too.

George was a very modest player though, he'd describe himself as a bit of a poacher and say things like "I just used to hang around the goalkeeper and wait for them to drop the ball so I could tap it in". But he was a far better player than he'd let you believe.

The common portrayal of your partnership is that there was almost a brotherly bond between the two of you. What was your relationship like with him off the pitch?

It was good, we were very close on and off the pitch and I was round at his family's house in Boliver's Road near Acton Town station a lot in the early days at Brentford. I even went out with his sister for a couple of years.

I think George adapted to League football quicker than I did after coming out of the Forces and it wasn't long before George Stobbart and Frank Dudley were looking over their shoulders.

What were they both like as forwards?

They were both very good, experienced players, but a lot older, at least ten years older than myself. Stobbart had played for Newcastle in the top flight, and I remember everyone knew him when we went up to play at St. James Park in the FA Cup in 1955. I played alongside George that day and he scored a goal but we lost three-two.

You scored on your debut, in a two-all draw at Shrewsbury in 1954, did you find it easy to adapt to life as a first-teamer?
It wasn't as big a step up as it was when I went into the reserves. Adapting from being a junior and making the jump to playing with far more experienced players was very difficult, something that's still the same today I would imagine. I remember my first game for the reserves more than I do my first team debut. We played Luton who were a very good side at the time, they had some very good players. Gordon Turner went on to play for England and score the most goals in his club's history and Michael Cullen went on to play for Scotland eventually. At the time they were nobodies like myself, but they were very tough opposition.

How would you describe yourself as a player?
That's really hard for me to say, I really don't like judging myself. I was just a goal-scorer really an out and out striker.

That's being a bit too modest surely, just one look at your goal-scoring record at Brentford [153 goals in 262 League games] shows what a prolific striker you were. You must have been a very special player to have earned stats like those?
Well I'd always played up front, even as a kid and I loved scoring goals. I really didn't care if I played well in a wider sense as long as I got a goal or two. Back then you couldn't get substituted, if you started you were on for ninety minutes, which made you more complacent as a player. Today if you play below par you'd get swapped for somebody else, that just didn't happen then, but it did give you more time to redeem yourself. If I wasn't having a good game there was always a chance to step it up a gear near the end and nick a goal.

But I suppose my biggest strength was that I had two good feet, everyone thought I was left footed, but I was actually right footed. If I took a penalty I'd always use my right. Players are studied in far more detail these days and if I'd played today people would have realised that I used to swap feet and work the ball a lot, which must have contributed to getting more goals.

If you can shoot with either foot it gives you far more of an advantage, you can strike at goal without having to use up time and switch the ball to your stronger side. Even strikers like Shearer and Owen have a preferred foot, but they'd get more goals if they could get a shot in no matter where the ball was; saving a fraction of a second is all-important. That was a big help for me.

You say you were always an out and out striker, but didn't Bill Dodgin play you out on the wing for a few games in the early days?
Yes he did actually, but only for a few matches. I was six feet tall and had a bit of pace so I guess he thought I may be able to do a decent job down the left, but I always felt out of the game stuck over there.

In those days a player's position was rigid, a winger would be told to stay wide and hug the touch-line and stay there. When I first joined the club I used to watch Jackie Goodwin and he would never be allowed to cut inside, his role was just to go up and down the line, beat his man and get a cross in.

You were asked to play a lot of friendlies and midweek leagues matches under the new Griffin Park floodlights in your era, if the goals you scored in those matches were included in your club record, your figures would be even more impressive wouldn't they?

I did score a lot of goals in those games yes, I remember scoring five goals against Vienna one night. Brentford had a good team, we were capable of taking most sides on in a one off game. I really used to like the white balls they used for the floodlight games, they were really good, better than the light ones they use today I think.

I got a fair few goals in The London Combination League too, that was for the reserves and players coming back from injuries. We'd often find ourselves playing against some of the best players in the Capital, and in most cases, these game used to provide a better class of opposition than our League games. Chelsea, Spurs and Arsenal were all included and some of the games could draw in a decent crowd too.

You must have just escaped having to use the old-fashioned kind of lace-up balls?

When I first joined Brentford we were still using them but things changed for the better while I was in the Army, the balls and boots became more modern and far better for the players, but I do remember having to use those old-fashioned ones too.

The structure of the Football League must have made it a frustrating time for clubs and players alike because only one team got promoted. Today's play-off set-up means that even a team finishing the season in sixth place can still achieve promotion. Do you find it annoying that after going so close three years on the trot and scoring a shed-load of goals for the club, that you never achieved promotion at Griffin Park?

To tell you the truth I don't think clubs were really too concerned about what league they were playing in. I wouldn't go as far a to say that they weren't bothered, but Brentford were getting crowds of around 18,000 in the Third Division South and there wasn't an awful lot more money to be made even if they did go up. The huge incentives for clubs and players simply weren't there, you've got to remember what a completely different era that was for football.

I was earning £18 a week at Brentford, whereas if I'd moved to Arsenal I would have only earned £2 more. The rules said that's all we could earn, it was

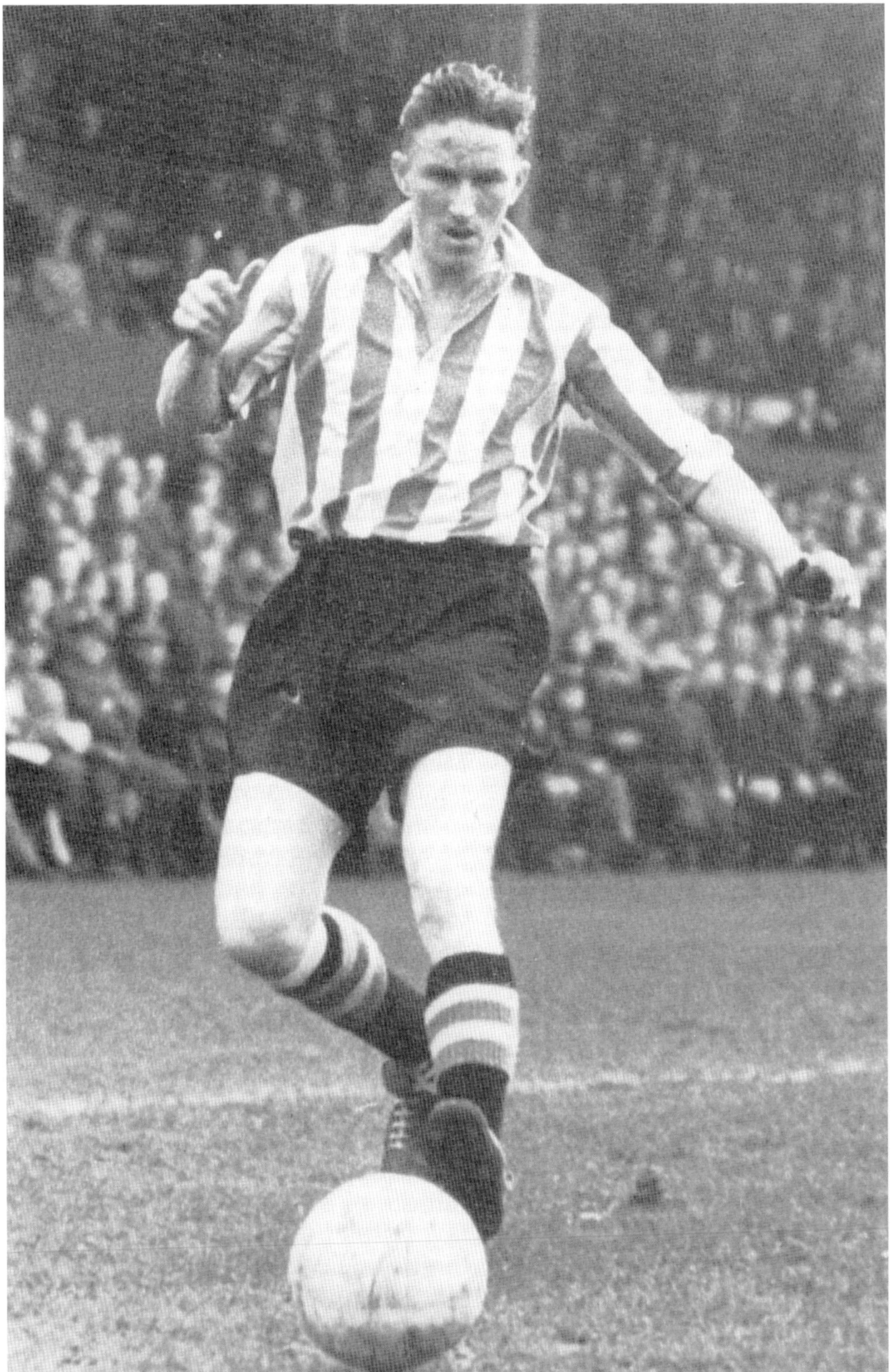

as simple as that. I never, ever remember a manager talking about the league tables or about how important it was for the club that we got promoted. As a professional you obviously wanted to play at the best level possible, but there wasn't any urgency or drive about winning the league every season.

At the beginning of the season there was never a pep talk to rally the players about going up. When I moved to QPR I felt that the manager, Alec Stock, was more focused, but it still wasn't the be-all and end-all.

So there was no bonus to incentivize the players to win promotion?

Well there was but it wasn't much money, I think I got something like £76 the season we finished third in the league, which was a joke really when we had twenty thousand people watching us every week. Yes there was a bonus but it wasn't enough to be at the forefront of your mind every week. I really can't get my head round the kind of rewards the lads are paid these days, I doubt they can either if they're honest.

A lot of players are earning £250,000 a month nowadays, they can't know what to do with it, really, they just can't spend that kind of money. I think it's going full circle now, they're earning so much that their incentive goes, the hunger dies. No wonder some of these top managers struggle to control their dressing rooms when everyone who plays for them is a multi-millionaire.

George Francis and yourself were dubbed 'The Terrible Twins' which seems a bit harsh, you weren't terrible at all were you?

[Laughs] The press gave us that name because they thought we terrorised defenders, but we did score a lot of goals between us! But then again, I think strikers from that era scored more goals than these days, there seemed to be a lots more goals around. My record worked out to around two goals every three games.

Opposition managers must have been well aware of the threat yourself and George Francis posed, did they tell their defenders to try and nobble you early on do you think?

Well I'm not sure they did know too much about us you know. The managers would have known we could score but there didn't seem to be the highly organised scouting and reporting that goes on today. We were never briefed about other team's style of play or the strengths and weaknesses of individual players from opposing teams, so I can only assume it was the same at other clubs.

There is so much more information available today, the name of every goal scorer is flashed up almost live on the television today, there are in-depth charts and tables on every player in the League. There was nothing like that then. Brentford's style of play caught a few sides out too, we were one of only a few sides using two out and out strikers at that time, which some sides struggled to cope with.

You were both in amazing form during the 1958-59 season, of Brentford's season tally of eighty-three goals, you two scored sixty-one of them. Your personal total was thirty-seven. Other clubs must have come in for you around that stage?
We were both playing very well that season, the team was playing good football and confidence was really high, it was an exciting time. Other teams did come in for me, yes, but there didn't seem much point in moving to be honest. There wasn't any more money to be made from playing in the First Division and when Sheffield Wednesday bid £20,000 for me I simply said that I didn't want to move all the way up there for a £2 per week rise.

It was the same when Norwich came in for me, I think they offered £12,000 and Newcastle made a few noises about wanting me too. But you also have to realise that you could still get picked to play for England if you were playing in the Third Division South, there were three full internationals from our division around that time.

It was acceptable to be a good player outside the top flight. It was common for a player to stay at one club throughout their whole career, and the England selectors didn't seem to downgrade a player if their team fell on tougher times. John Atyeo at Bristol City was their top goal-scorer, he played a massive amount of games and scored loads of goals, but he was still picked for England as a Third Division player. Then there was Reg Matthews of Coventry and England, although he eventually went to Chelsea, he was another to play for his country from our division.

So you see there wasn't really a stigma attached to being a lower league player, if you were happy at your club, you could stay and still get on in the game, and without the possibility of earning much more anywhere else, that's why there was much more loyalty and long-service in the game.

So you don't resent not making much money out of the game?
Not really, it was the same for all of us, even the superstars like Stanley Matthews had to catch the tram to the ground on match-days, I think it made the game far more friendlier and equal. I got a benefit game for Brentford, which earned me a few bob, they organised a game with Glasgow Celtic at Griffin Park and we beat them two-nil. I got a cheque for about £600.

What's your memory like for goals, do you remember many of them?
I hardly remember any of them if I'm being honest. I can vaguely recall one or two, like my debut goal at Shrewsbury, and I remember scoring in the last couple of minute against QPR at Griffin Park in 1960 to settle a two-nil win.

Did you set yourself goal targets at the start of the season?
Oh no, nothing like that at all. Obviously I wanted to score every time I played but there were no big prizes up for grabs, the motivation to set targets for yourself wasn't there, it didn't really cross my mind. I guess you could call me unambitious, but that was just what football was like at the time, it was a far more simple game and there was far less pressure involved.

Malcolm McDonald replaced Bill Dodgin as manager in 1957, what did you think of the new man?
I had a lot of respect for Malcolm, I knew he'd been a good player for Brentford, and although I never played with him, you could tell he could still play a bit when he joined in during training. But Malcolm definitely used to favour fellow Scots, and he brought a few down to play for Brentford who didn't really settle in too well, players like Charlie McInally and Johnny Hales.

What were the local Derbies with QPR like at the time, were they heated affairs?
Well, we obviously liked to beat them and vice versa, but I don't remember them being particularly dirty. I know that we had a really good record against them and we beat them most of the time. Mark Lazarus, who like myself played for both clubs in his career, was playing for QPR at the time and he used to have a good battle with the Brentford defence. Ironically my first game for Rangers after being transferred there was against Brentford and I scored, which felt a bit odd I must admit.

So how did the move to our arch-rivals come about?
To this day I don't know why they decided to sell me and George [Francis] to QPR, but they obviously needed the money. I remember walking out of Griffin Park after training one day and the club secretary, Dennis Piggot, and manager, Malcolm McDonald, called me back and told me that they'd had an offer from Loftus Road and they wanted to sell me.

I wasn't told that they were in for George too, my transfer came first and they made a move for George a little while afterwards. It wasn't as if I got any money out of the transfer either. I genuinely didn't want to go and I wish I'd stayed at Brentford, but once you are told they want you to go you know that you're not wanted any more. Maybe they had to pay off a bill or something because they almost begged me to go. Brentford were a certainty for relegation after that I thought, which is what happened in 1962. But then the season after I left Ron Blindell joined the board at Griffin Park from Plymouth and I think he put a lot of money into the club.

Brentford started buying good players again, men like Johnnie Dicks from West Ham, Billy McAdams from Leeds and Johnny Brooks from Chelsea, what a

March 1961: Jim Towers clatters into the 'keeper during a nil-nil draw with Barnsley

good player Johnny was. In 1963 The Bees went back up as Champions.

George Francis didn't settle at Rangers did he?
No he was back at Brentford within a season. George was a bit unlucky really because for some reason he wasn't in from the start and Rangers didn't use us as a partnership as we were at Brentford. He lost out to other strikers in the squad and decided to move back.

What was QPR like compared to Brentford when you switched in 1961?
Very, very similar, probably a bit better run than Brentford and Alec Stock trained the players harder, but there weren't many differences.

By all accounts you had a pretty ferocious shot on you, do you remember when you broke a goalie's hand while scoring?
Bernard Streten his name was if my memory serves me. He was a former international who had played for Luton as a professional.

How big a part did Johnny Rainford play in your and George Francis' goal-scoring success?
John was a very good player, he was ahead of his time and very good on the ball. He used to play just behind the front two and he did set up a lot of goals for us. Strikers weren't expected to get back and help defend or do anything more than make a nuisance of themselves up front then, so John Rainford had a lot more work to do than us.

Which other team-mates would you single out from Brentford?
Kenny Coote was different class, in my opinion he was the best player Brentford has ever had. I'd seen some of the great Brentford First Division defenders in action, people like Archie Macaulay and Billy Scott, but to me Ken was better than anyone else I saw or played with.

Ken and myself got picked to play for the London XI and he was the best player in that side too. The side was made up of the best players in London, including the First Division clubs, and Ken would still stand out. Ken got picked for the FA XI one season too, which was the equivalent of winning a cap for your country at the time I would say.

So you feel Ken Coote deserved to play at the top level in the game?
Without a doubt, it was like having an extra man with Ken in the side. But players just didn't move around as much as they do now and Ken was happy to stay at Brentford.

Were you close to Ken Coote?
Yes, he was my best mate at the club. We were always round each other's

houses and we used to go out for a drink together right up until he died.

What was the standard of refereeing like in your era in your view?
Oh they were terrible, the referees were so bad in those days… Everybody used to win at home back then! They had an impossible job really, they had no back-up and it was almost unheard of to send a player off. They were like schoolmasters really, but we knew they were poor and influenced by the crowd, so we just had to get on with it.

What do you consider you proudest achievement at the club?
Scoring those thirty-seven goals in 1958-59 I would say, I really enjoyed myself that season.

CULT BEES AND LEGENDS VOLUME TWO

Francis Joseph

131

Francis Joseph is the first person to admit how fortunate he was to have played in the same Brentford side as the iconic midfield trio of Stan Bowles, Terry Hurlock and Chris Kamara - it must have been a striker's dream come true to feed off that kind of creative flair. But the finishing prowess of Joseph shouldn't be underestimated, despite the fabulous service - Francis' goals-per-game stats are right up there with some of the greatest strikers in the club's history.

At the time Francis Joseph arrived, Brentford were in the position of being able to demand the best players from their fellow Third Division rivals, and before the tables were turned, Wimbledon had little choice in allowing their starlet to transfer from Plough Lane to Griffin Park. Over the next two seasons the former Womble amassed a stunning fifty-goal haul.

Unfortunately fans look back at that period as a time when Brentford underachieved massively, Fred Callaghan's side possessed all the ingredients to mount a successful promotion campaign, and perhaps if it hadn't been for the injury to Tony Mahoney in 1982-83, things may have panned out differently.

Joseph offers a philosophical insight into that time and the leg-breaks that interrupted what would have been a longer and more fruitful Brentford career.

Both you and your brother, Roger, played for Brentford - you obviously came from a very talented football family?

Potentially there could have been four footballing brothers in the Joseph family, our other two brothers used to think they could play a bit too, but they didn't make the grade. My mother and father encouraged us all but I never thought I would actually become a professional.

Early on I thought football was just a fun activity, I didn't really take the game too seriously until I was about sixteen when I was invited to try out for Willesden Football Club. I played for them for the best part of a season, then it all kicked off for me. I was also playing for Chalk Hill Youth Club near Wembley, and during the course of that season, I scored almost seventy goals. I found that people then started to sit up and take note.

A guy called Viv Evans at Wealdstone then invited me down to play in their youth side, which ironically is the same side I coach today. Then Alan Batsford at Hillingdon Borough signed me and he really got me believing I could make it as a pro. I remember Alan saying to me after a game one day, "if you're still playing for me this time next season I will kill you, you are going to be a professional." Well, I'm still alive!

So you became confident that it was only a matter of time before a Football League club came along and snap you up?

Well, let's put it this way, I believed it would happen for me or it wouldn't happen for me in equal measures. I knew that if I kept scoring goals people would become more and more interested, I was obviously still learning the game, but all the raw ingredients were there.

So you must have been delighted when Wimbledon gave you a chance as a full time footballer?

I really was, I loved my time at Wimbledon and couldn't speak more highly about the club or their fans. I remember being really emotional when I left to join Brentford, I was like a kid leaving school going out into the big wide world. I did a lot of growing up at Plough Lane.

How crazy was it at Wimbledon in those early days?

Dario Gradi was the manager at the time and Dave Bassett was his assistant… it was amazing. The training was the most full-blooded grounding any young player could have wished for, not for the faint-hearted. I learned a lot from Dario. The impact that man has had on English football. His record in the game and what he's achieved for Crewe speaks for itself. I was lucky enough to play for him again up at Crewe later in my career and I've adopted as many of Dario's disciplines in my training with the kids at Wealdstone.

It was a totally professional set-up at Wimbledon and the coaches instilled a winning mentality in us all. Being second to the ball, losing out in a header, missing out in a sprint to the ball… none of that was tolerated. After six months or so at Plough Lane Dario moved on to manage Crystal Palace. Dave Bassett then took over, which produced Wimbledon's famous march through the leagues.

Did you have any idea when you joined that Wimbledon Football Club would go on to play in the top flight?

Absolutely. The passion of the players and supporters was fantastic, they deserved their success. Just look at the superb efforts of the fans at AFC Wimbledon today, in my view they are beautiful people and fanatical about their club.

If they could have only got their new stadium in Surrey then I'm sure Wimbledon, as they were, would have got the crowds that were needed to continue the success, maybe that day will come again, who knows?

Brentford fans sat up and took notice of you after Wimbledon staged a memorable second half come-back at Griffin Park in April 1982. Two-nil down at half time you came back to win three-two and Francis Joseph was on fire scoring two of them. Do you remember that night?

I certainly do! The players were all down in the dumps as we went in at the break because we hadn't played too badly in the first half, but Dave Bassett rallied us. I was whining like a little baby to the other players, "just give me the ball…" I kept moaning. I often think that night was the making of me as a football player.

Did Brentford come in for you straight after that match at Griffin Park?
Pretty quickly yeah, but I had a chance of going to Millwall too. I must admit that the Millwall fans' reputation played a big part in me not signing for them, I knew that if I had a couple of bad games for The Lions there'd be a good chance that I'd be found hanging from a lamp-post outside The Den.

So how did you find Brentford after your Wimbledon 'apprenticeship', did you feel at home straight away?
Not straight away, no, but I knew I'd joined another fantastic club, another family club, only much bigger than Wimbledon.

How did you find Fred Callaghan and Ron Harris compared to your previous bosses?
Fred was a wind-up merchant, he'd get on your back and gee you up to get the best out of his players, it was continuous. Fred could play a bit still too, everyone used to look at him and think 'big fat Fred' but he had a great touch still and you could tell that he'd been pretty good.

[Laughs] As for Ron he would wind you up almost as much as Fred in training, but then he'd kick you too! Ron was still playing at the time and woe betide any player who tried to get past him on the training pitch because he certainly didn't get the 'Chopper' nickname for no good reason. Gary Roberts, Chris Kamara and Stan Bowles were his favourites, he just loved kicking those three.

You joined a side jammed packed with real characters didn't you?
Yes I played with a fantastic bunch at Brentford, not only people like Terry Hurlock and Stan Bowles, but Gary Roberts, Terry Rowe, Keith Cassells, Terry Bullivant and Paddy Roche too. They were all great guys at Brentford to be honest.

You got off to an absolute flier at Griffin Park; the Francis Joseph - Tony Mahoney - Gary Roberts combination up front seemed to click from the off. The Bees won their opening game to the 1982-83 campaign five-one against Bristol Rovers and in the following weeks the three of you were scoring for fun. Could you have had a better start at a new club?
It couldn't have got much better really, but I knew things would click way before the opening day. I remember we played Northampton in a pre-season friendly that year at the old Wimbledon training ground and we scored nine or ten past them... I got five and I thought 'here we go!' The service to the front players was so good, it was a striker's dream.

But Gary Roberts was one greedy git I can tell you, if that guy was on a hat-trick there was no way on earth that you were going to get a pass from him. It's no exaggeration to say that sometimes out on the pitch all the other players genuinely wanted to kill him. When we got back to the changing room after some games he would try and laugh it all off by offering to buy everyone a beer in the bar, but even after I'd taken a drink off him, I could have still murdered the bloke!

So, Gary Roberts aside, the superior service you received at Brentford must have helped you develop as a striker?
The service at Wimbledon was good, but it was a different type of delivery. I'm not knocking the way Wimbledon played as it was good for my career, but at Brentford there was a lot more imagination and creativity. At Plough Lane it was all about determination and bottle, if a player didn't have those two, then you were no use to them. Then, if you made a mistake, your clothes would get burned in the dressing room.

But surely the Brentford style was more enjoyable for a player, having Stan Bowles or Terry Hurlock threading lovely balls through for you to run on to rather than the blood and thunder, pumping the long-ball down the channels for you to scratch, punch or bite your way to winning?
I know what you mean, but I feel I still owe that style of football an awful lot and we can't forget how successful it became. To be honest I guess you could call the Wimbledon way thuggery, at Plough Lane the mantra was 'if you come into my house and want a fight, boy are you gonna get one'. But Wimbledon and their brand of football prepared me for everything that could be thrown at me as a footballer.

You scored twenty-six goals in your first season at Brentford, that was some going wasn't it?
I think I should have scored about sixty that year. No lie, I used to look around me on the football pitch and think 'f***ing hell', am I lucky to be on the same pitch as these guys or what?' I used to rate myself as a player, but I was sometimes overwhelmed by the pedigree around me.

Few would argue with you over the pedigree of that team, so what was its undoing, why did the side under-achieve so badly?
I've often thought about that but I don't think it was as simple as having a dodgy defence. To be fair I don't think the players at the back were that bad. More than anything in that first season I think we missed Danis Salman's pace at full-back, and although Danis wasn't a big guy, he could win his headers too. I remember we used to have some right battles in training.

So for most of my first season we had Alan Whitehead at centre-back, he was the big lump alongside Jim McNichol; neither of them would shirk anything. Then there was Barry Tucker and Graham Wilkins at right and left backs, but if

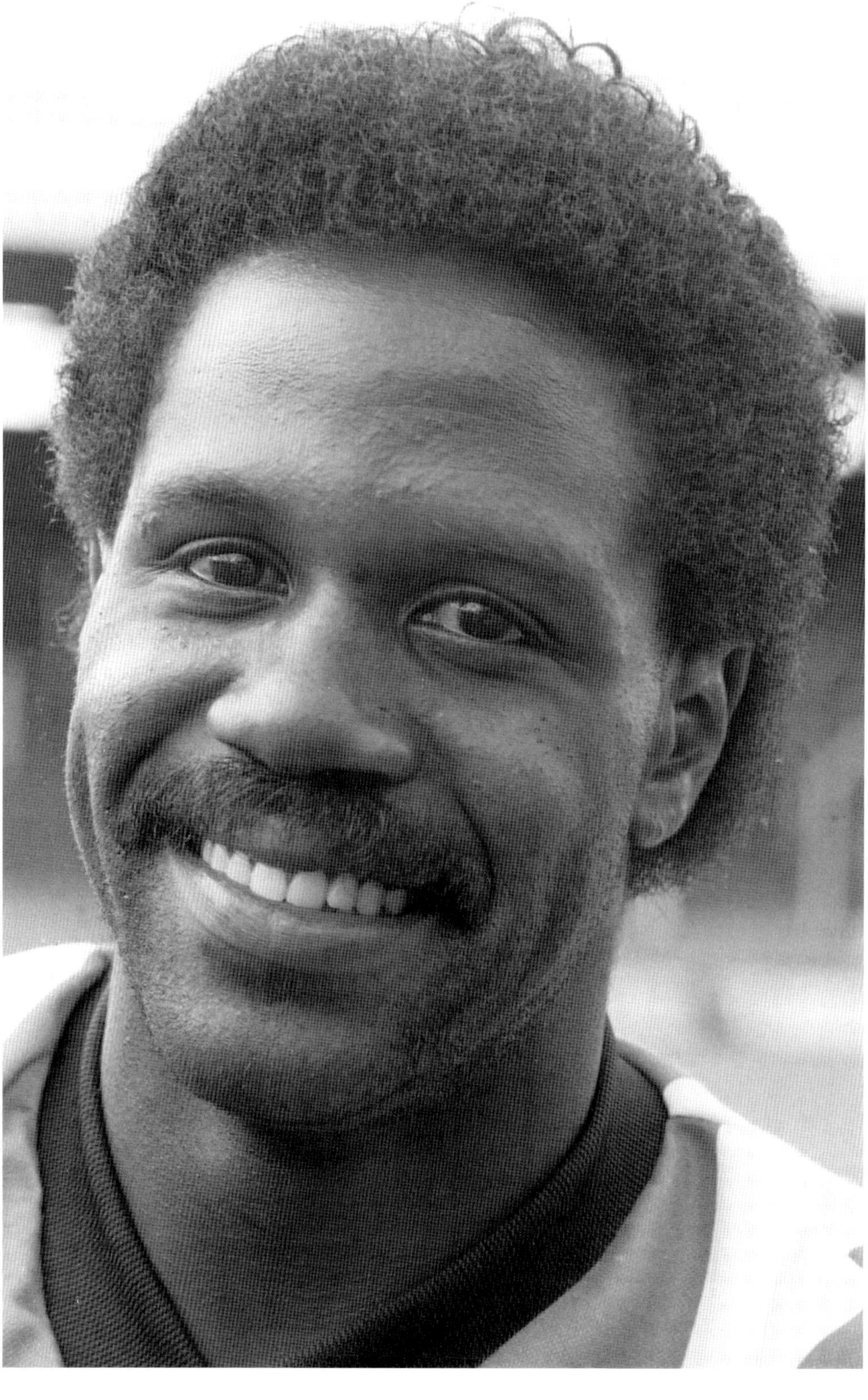

either of the full-backs got injured, young Terry Rowe would come in. [Laughs out loud] Virtually everything that Terry Rowe knew about tackling had been taught to him by Ron Harris, so boy could he tackle!

We used to call Terry 'The Undertaker' because he used to bury wingers. I thought Terry Rowe did really well coming in to the side, which upset people like Graham Wilkins because he didn't automatically get his place back when he was fit again. For a seventeen-year-old kid I thought Terry was absolutely marvellous, in fact, in my time as a footballer, I've only seen one or two better at that age.

Another pivotal moment in your first season at the club was the injury to Tony Mahoney. Before breaking his leg your strike-partner had bagged fifteen goals before Christmas. How did you get on with Tony and how big a blow was the injury to the rest of the side?

Like a lot of successful striking partnerships the players don't always see eye to eye. The fans certainly saw the goals we were scoring during the early part of the 82-83 season, but I'm not sure quite how many of them saw the rows that myself and Tony shared too. We'd run up to one another to congratulate each other whenever we scored a goal, but if either of us missed a chance and the other one was in a better goal scoring position, boy did we bicker. If he used to get a goal, it made me try even harder to get one myself and I'm sure it was the same in reverse. But his loss was a big blow to the side for sure.

Tony didn't just break his leg, he shattered it in three places during that FA Cup tie at Swindon. Do you remember the incident?

Absolutely, I'll never forget it. I was running right next to him when it happened. The reason why the injury was so bad in my opinion was because Tony was really frustrated during that match, things weren't going the way he would have liked and he wasn't happy at all.

I remember I'd told him to calm down a couple of times and the challenge that he went in for, the one that caused the break, was absolutely crazy I thought. But then again, every prolific striker in a professional league has got to have an aggressive edge.

Even mild mannered, calm and polite men off the pitch need to turn in to something completely different on the field of play if they are going to get to the top in the game. It's a hard game played by hard men, no matter what it looks like from the sidelines at times.

So the tackle that did the damage to Tony Mahoney wasn't caused by a malicious defender at all?

No, not as I saw it. There were times in matches where I went in for similar challenges too, if your form or luck isn't great during a game, going in for a sixty-forty challenge stacked in a defender's favour, then winning the ball and getting a clean run on goal, can turn your game around. But at other times you can misjudge things completely and end up getting really hurt. But that's football.

As a team-mate and fellow professional it must have been really disturbing to see Mahoney in so much agony?
Of course, it's the injury that every player dreads, but you can't let it affect your game otherwise you may as well walk off the pitch. I've witnessed a fair few bad injuries on the pitch, but again, that's football.

Keith Cassells, or 'Rosie' as he was nicknamed, was then brought in from Southampton by Fred Callaghan as your new partner, was it a similar relationship with him too?
All professional strikers have a selfish, nasty streak. As I've said, you can't make it in the game unless you have that edge and Keith was just the same. The best example of how determined and hungry the forwards at Brentford were to score goals happened down at Exeter at the end of my first season.

We were winning seven-one down at their place and there was still twenty minutes left on the clock; Keith Cassells had got two, Chris Kamara had got two and I had got two. That greedy so-and-so Roberts had just made it seven.

There were three of us queuing up for hat-tricks and if Gary Roberts had used his brains he could have set us all up and probably joined us in the scrap for the match ball. Time and time again we were crying out for the ball to be pulled back to us or for it to be squared to the player in space, but he kept going for glory himself. Again, we wanted to kill the guy. It was surreal, we'd just murdered a side seven-one on their own patch and there were three miserable players prowling round the dressing room wearing faces like they'd just lost the game by the same score-line. But we'd come to expect that from Gaspin' Gary Roberts.

Can you explain to those younger Brentford fans exactly why people used to call Gary Roberts ' Gaspin'?
Easy, because he was always gaspin' for a beer. But believe me, I had a few other nicknames for the guy too, but I'd better keep them to myself because he's a policeman now.

Do you remember getting sent off up at Doncaster in 1982? Brentford were four-one behind, then down to ten men after your dismissal, but still managed to fight back and square the match four-all.
That was the first time I'd ever been sent off. I remember the game wasn't going our way at all and it seemed that the referee was giving all the decisions to the home side. I remember Tony Mahoney was having a right go at the ref

after he'd blown up yet again to give Rovers a free kick. I said to my partner, "you're wasting your time, this guy's a right homer, he's gonna give us nothing mate..." The referee glared at me as the game restarted, then a minute later, after I'd gone in for a nonsense tackle, he booked me.

"What the hell was that for ref?" I screamed at the guy. He was having a laugh. Then shortly afterwards, I bumped into one of the Doncaster defenders who decided to roll around the ground like a true continental prima-donna. After telling the guy to get up I looked round to see a red card being waved in my face. It was a joke, I just walked past the referee towards the dugout shaking my head and telling the bloke what I thought about him.

Amazingly, even with the referee against us all afternoon, we still managed to fight back and draw four-all. Bob Booker got the equaliser right near the end.

Booker was a great servant of the club, did you get on well with Bob?
Everyone got on with Bob. He's an unbelievably nice bloke. He was a very accomplished player too, I got the feeling that the fans didn't always see quite how good he really was or appreciate what they had at the club sometimes.

Bob had been at Brentford for a fair few years and in my opinion his move away from Griffin Park was the making of him as a player. I wouldn't say that he'd been at Brentford for too long, but sometimes a move away and a new start elsewhere can give a long-serving player a huge boost in confidence and energy.

Bob really made a name for himself at Sheffield United, where I teamed up with him again in the late 80s. I remember after a home game at Bramall Lane one afternoon the physio, Derek French, came over to me and told me he had something to show me. I must admit that I was more interested in making sure that no bugger stole my piping hot bath than in following Derek out of the changing room, but when I stepped out into the corridor I was faced by a beaming Bob Booker. It was really nice to hook up with him again and Bob became a hero at the club, captaining them in the top flight too.

So talk me through the best Brentford midfield in living memory?
Stan Bowles was the best player I'd ever seen in my life, I remember watching him as a child, so to be playing with him was something pretty special. Chris Kamara; tall, skinny with great energy. He could really tackle and alongside Terry Hurlock you had a superb partnership in the middle. Terry Hurlock, TERRY HURLOCK, he could go through brick walls. He was like a cave man carrying a sledgehammer, a Pikey Chav, but very dangerous. But what a nice man too.

They were tough guys those two together, if the going got tough on the pitch those guys would get involved, but first and foremost they wanted to play good football and succeeded in my view. They both were rewarded with big moves after Brentford, which proved what good players they were.

CULT BEES AND LEGENDS VOLUME TWO

Francis Joseph lets fly at goal watched by fellow Brentford legend Chris Kamara

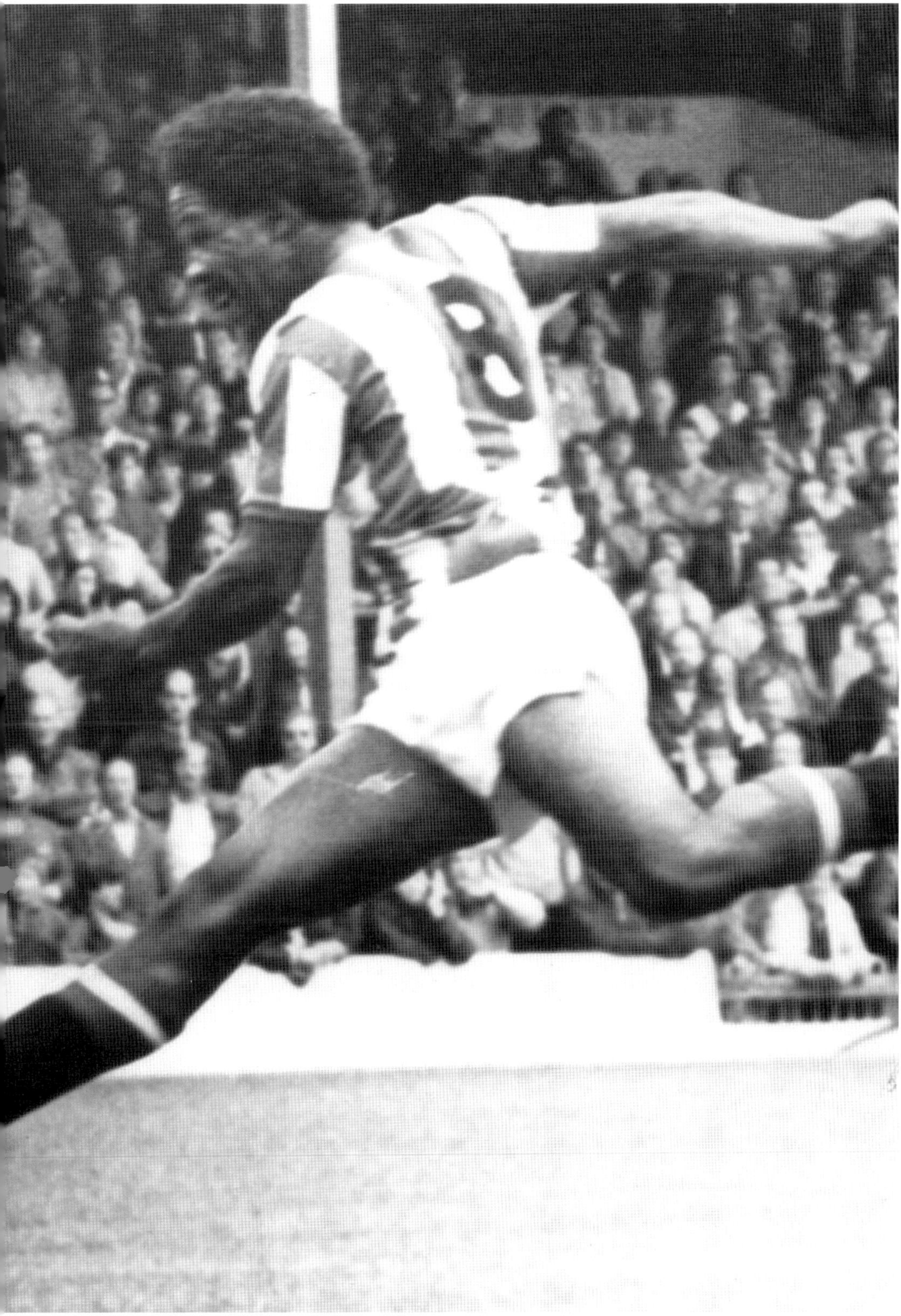

Now that Chris Kamara is a minor TV celebrity he seems to have wiped the time he spent at Brentford from his memory. I've spoken to him a couple of times in recent years and he seems reluctant to talk about his days at Griffin Park, why do you think that is?

To be fair, I can probably understand it from a player's point of view, but for a fan it must seem a bit of an insult to your club. Perhaps when you're in the media you have to be more of a big time Charlie and only talk about your time in the top flight rather than the seasons you had to spend in the lower divisions, but ultimately helped get him to the top in the first place.

Brentford was probably Chris' launching pad, okay his best memories from a great career were probably recorded at Sheffield United and Leeds, but he was Brentford captain for a while and he made a reputation as a quality, consistent player at Griffin Park. Chris should have good memories about the place.

Goalies Paddy Roche and Trevor Swinburne. Were either any good?

No disrespect to Trevor but I'd have picked Paddy ahead of him all day long. I'm not saying that because Paddy was my room mate on away trips, in fact he used to say bugger all for hours on end, but he was the complete pro both on the training pitch and during the match.

I thought Paddy made very few mistakes for Brentford. You should have seen the state of his car though, what a state! You would never have thought he had played for Manchester United for all that time, it was like his mobile wardrobe. His digs couldn't have had any storage space because it looked like he carried all his worldly possessions around with him in the back of his motor.

Apart from having to share your hotel room with Paddy on those long trips north, what was travelling away like in general in that era?

A great laugh, we used to play a lot of cards on the coach journey, a game called Hearts. Terry Hurlock was always the first one on the coach because he lived just opposite the ground in Braemar Road and he'd have all the cards set up and ready for when the rest of us boarded. We were playing for money, but nothing silly, only a few quid here and there. Nobody made a killing. [Laughs] I always thought it was a great feeling walking off the bus with an extra few quid of my team mates' money in my pocket.

So, if the player's gambling didn't get out of hand, did the drinking?

Not as far as I remember, well, nothing too bad. Wednesday night was always my cut-off if we didn't have a midweek match, but if we had a Tuesday night game and won, most of the lads would go out and get lashed up.

There was no way you could go home and sleep, the adrenaline would be pumping for hours afterwards. Some days after training a few of the boys would go to The New Inn for lunch, the food in there was fantastic, so I guess we'd have a couple of pints, but that was it. Paddy Roche used to love it in that pub, for a skinny bloke he could really put his food away and he would often finish off Stan Bowles' lunch too because Stan had the appetite of a sparrow.

I remember Paddy had the most terrible wind problems though, he'd let rip after a meal and clear most of the pub out. But I'd say most weeks, Thursdays and Fridays were completely dry days.

Season 1982-83 may have been a disappointing league campaign, but the side certainly enjoyed a decent League Cup run. Wimbledon were seen off in the First Round, Blackburn Rovers were then knocked out at Ewood Park on aggregate, then Brentford were pitted against Swansea City who were a top flight side at the time. What do you remember of that run?

It was good to get one over my old team mates so quickly after leaving Plough Lane, even though I didn't score in either leg. Then we played really well to beat Blackburn, who were in the league above us, three-two at Griffin Park and held on for a nil-nil up at their place.

As you say, Swansea were in the equivalent of the Premier League at the time and had some cracking players; Ray Kennedy was still playing for them and John Toshack was the manager. We held them one-all at Griffin Park in front of over fifteen thousand fans, Gaspin' got our goal, then we went to their place and did them two-one.

Did the Brentford players consider the Swansea win a real upset?

I'm deadly serious when I tell you this, even though I know it's over twenty years ago now and you tend to look back at things through slightly rose-tinted glasses, but that Brentford side was capable of beating top flight sides on a regular basis I think. When all the players were on fire we were a match for anyone. Even Nottingham Forest, the Champions of Europe at the time, who we got in the Fourth Round, had to work their socks off to knock us out at The City Ground. For me, the Swansea City win wasn't a surprise.

Brentford were lucky with League Cup draws around that era, the following season we beat Charlton Athletic home and away in Round One, then were drawn against Liverpool in the next stage. What do you remember of the ties against The Reds?

Again, I thought we matched them pass for pass for most of the game, especially in the first game at Griffin Park. They were awarded a very dubious goal, Mike Robinson shoved Alan Whitehead off the ball, which the referee turned a blind eye to, then he was allowed to cross for Ian Rush to slot home.

That spurred us on though, not too long afterwards yours truly beat Sammy Lee and Phil Neal with a little shimmy to set up Gary Roberts who fired a screamer past Bruce Grobbelaar to make it one-all at half time.

If I'm totally honest I'd have to blame individual goalkeeping errors for a couple of the second half Liverpool goals. Trevor Swinburne spilled a couple of shots, which you couldn't afford to do with Rush and Robinson sniffing around in front of you, so we lost four-one on the night then four-nil at Anfield.

How did you rate your personal performances against Nottingham Forest and Liverpool, the two biggest sides in the country at the time?
It was good to be on the same pitch as people like Kenny Dalglish and Graeme Souness when they were at their peak, but I wasn't happy with the way I'd played at all. If they don't score a goal, strikers rate their performances on either shots on target, or assists that help other players score. But looking back, I can't recall a single effort I had that went near the goal.

Forest's Colin Todd had me in his pocket and I was very disappointed in my performance. As a young ambitious professional you crave those opportunities to put yourself in the shop window or scrap it out with the best defenders in the land and it's no exaggeration to say that I had trouble sleeping for almost a week after the Forest defeat.

That night I have to admit that I didn't care about the team's performance, I was gutted for myself because I was shocking. I scored two goals in the next game against Wrexham though which got the Forest match out of my system.

A lot of Brentford fans still look back at the 1982-83 season as the year that if Brentford had gone up and kept the squad together, then we may have gone on to the top flight again. Is that the way you see it?
I felt sorry for Fred Callaghan I really did, I agree, I think that side was so close to achieving big things for the club. It was a missed opportunity alright. Finishing tenth that season wasn't good enough because we had the potential to finish in the top two and win promotion without any shadow of a doubt.

People can run out all kinds of excuses; Tony Mahoney breaking his leg, Danis Salman's injury, the suspension of both Kamara and Hurlock at crucial times during the season, but I think that's all nonsense. We should have still gone up. There were other decent footballers in the wings who used to come in to the side, players like Paul Walker.

I used to think Paul was a super little player and most of the time he didn't get a look in. If we could have gone up that season the club would have gone from strength to strength. In my view no Brentford side since has matched the skill of that squad.

I also remember we just missed out on winning a big pot of money that had been put up by Capital Radio for the first London side to score a hundred goals in league and cup matches. Wimbledon had a midweek game and notched up goal one hundred to grab the loot just days before we smashed Exeter seven-one.

Callaghan seemed unable to build on that potential and he paid with his job midway through the 1983-84 season. A six-nil mauling at Southend United, followed shortly afterwards by the infamous 'three-one up at Gillingham with eleven minutes to go but we still managed to lose five-three' FA Cup game, put the nails in his managerial coffin.

[Puts his head in his hands] God I remember that game at Gillingham! How did we ever lose that match? We were comfortable, and I remember I'd been roasting Steve Bruce all afternoon, as I did every time I played him. Brentford were cruising into Round Four.

The problem was, Fred had brought in Ian Bolton from Watford and he had an absolute nightmare in the closing stages of the match. Tony Cascarino was all over him and every time the ball went near Ian Bolton they scored. At the end of the game Terry Hurlock walked straight over to Ian and told the bloke exactly how shit he thought he was. The result was a real slap in the face because for eighty minutes we'd played really well.

Frank McLintock was unveiled as the new Bees manager shortly afterwards, how did he differ from his predecessor?

I got on well with both Fred and Frank to be honest. The biggest difference I can remember was that you could have a falling out with Frank in training or after a game and he wouldn't hold a grudge. The next morning it would be all brushed under the carpet, Frank was mature like that.

With Fred, if you had a falling out, he'd let it brew and brew. Frank was a more understanding individual I thought, but with the same desire to win. The Frank McLintock - John Docherty manager and assistant partnership proved to be a successful one a year or so later at Millwall, unfortunately, in hindsight, they got the roles the wrong way round at Brentford. Another thing to note was the fact that Frank would drop me from the side from time to time where Fred would always include me no matter what.

Frank and myself would have some blazing rows and be right in each other's faces, I even walked out on training on one or two occasions and Terry Hurlock had to come and find me in a pub in Kilburn to talk me back round and calm me down. But Frank's ability to recover and be calm with me afterwards was excellent and I've tried to take that quality on board now that I'm coaching. In fact I haven't really got a bad word to say about any of the managers and assistants I had at Brentford, apart from Ron Harris, who was a right tight git!

You then had a traumatic period of injuries, breaking your leg twice in as many seasons, the second time less than two games after a nine-month rehabilitation. Did you ever think your career was over during that period?

Never, I knew I'd fight my way back. The late club physio, Eddie Lyons, was by my side the whole way, he was a real character. The players only used to train in the mornings back then, but Eddie would stay on with me every afternoon to help me with my exercises, then when I was able to do light jogging again, he'd be running along behind me round and round the training ground at Osterley.

What a great man Eddie was, and boy did he love his wife Iris. I wish I could find a woman I could love as much as I knew he loved her. [Laughs] He used to bore me stupid with his food stories though, every morning he'd come in and tell me what he'd had for dinner the night before; "Jo, my Iris cooked me a lovely Shepherd's Pie last night..." or, "you should have seen the roast I had yesterday..." I was a real ladies man at the time so perhaps Eddie was trying to persuade me it was time to settle down to some good home cooking?

How did the break happen, I'm sure something like that sticks vividly in your mind?
It was just one of those things really. I'd shaken off one defender and was moving inside the penalty area when I saw the Wigan defender, Steve Walsh, coming in to tackle me. I decided to shoot early, but as I let fly, my shin and the bottom of his studs impacted with the follow through. I probably shouldn't have gone for the shot in hindsight, but you have to go in brave, it was my job to score goals and take shots, so bottling out doesn't cross your mind.

I didn't know I'd broken my leg straight away, but when I tried to get back to my feet, boy was I in pain. It turned out to be a very awkward injury, not a clean break, that's why it took so long for me to come back and why the bone broke in the same place so soon after returning to the first team. The medical people should have broken it properly afterwards so the bone could knit together better and heal quicker.

It must have been a huge mental blow when your leg snapped again?
All I could think about was all that bloody swimming I'd have to do over again and all those Shepherd's pie stories I'd have to endure from Eddie. But I knew I'd be back, you go through torture the first month, but I was strong enough.

How about the medical support the club provided to help you recover?
It was adequate, but I feel the private treatment that I eventually needed should have been offered sooner than it was. Initially I went to the hospital where I had to queue up with everyone else. As a football player I should have gone private from day one, the NHS isn't the best route or quickest recovery for a pro. Frank sorted me out in the end and got me up to Harley Street.

But by that stage I'd been in plaster for more than two months, then the specialist told me he felt we needed to approach the problem in a different way. But when the cast came off and I was going round on crutches it really freaked me out, I was so scared that people would bump in to me that I

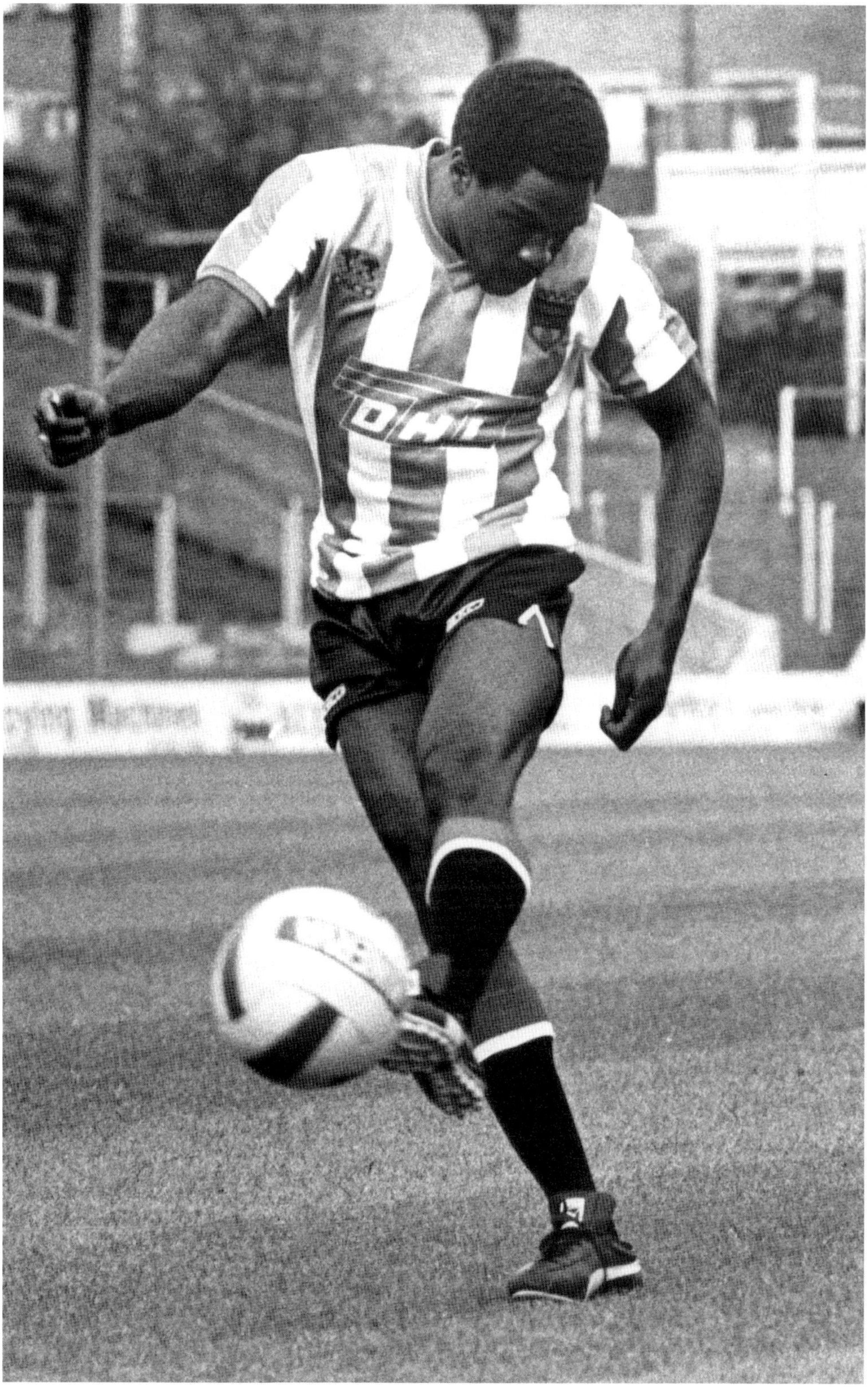

CULT BEES **AND** LEGENDS **VOLUME** TWO

couldn't leave the house for a week. I was even too frightened to go to the player's Christmas party that year.

Frank McLintock will always be remembered by Brentford fans for some very dodgy signings, for every Robbie Cooke there was an Ian Holloway or a Rowan Alexander. Do you agree with that?
Frank really screwed it up in the transfer market, a combination of letting too many good players go, then bringing in some substandard replacements. Some of his signings were good players though; Jamie Murray was okay, Bobby Fisher was good and Tom Finney was another one of those players that would crunch a forward all day long in the tackle, and another lovely bloke off the pitch too. The players I was most upset with were Rowan Alexander and Steve Butler, they were poor.

I remember Terry Hurlock telling me after training one afternoon that he'd been speaking to Frank about a new striker he was about to sign; a big, strapping Scottish centre-forward, somebody the manager was confident could replace the fifty goals I'd scored in my two seasons at the club.

So you can imagine our faces when five-foot-nothing Rowan turned up at training for the first time. It did make me think whether Frank had ever seen the player first hand or if he'd had a change of plan at the last moment and had bought somebody else instead. Don't get me wrong, Rowan was a nice boy who worked hard, very hard, but we needed a maturer player at that time.

Whenever I hit a bad pass during a match or in training I'd be mad with myself but could shrug it off quickly and get on with my game, but the way I saw things, if Rowan did the same, it seemed to affect his confidence badly.

The highlight of Frank's time at Brentford was the side's Wembley appearance in the Freight Rover Cup Final against Wigan in 1985. Being injured still, where did you watch the match?
I watched it down on the bench but the side didn't perform on the day and it was a horrible experience to be looking on with a busted leg. I felt sorry for my team mates because they were so shocking. But it was just one of those things. Robbie Cooke got a good goal, but then again, I thought Robbie was a very good striker. He's the Chief Scout for Everton Football Club these days.

You made your long awaited return to the side at the end of April 1986, scoring in a three-all draw at home to York City. Your brother, Roger, also scored in that game which was a new club record.
Roger had been with me at Brentford almost from day one. As soon as I signed I told Fred Callaghan that he should have a look at my brother. He had very good pace and recovery, Roger was a very good player. It was a great experience to have your brother as a team mate.

Then, just after you'd battled your way to full match fitness and had started scoring some goals again, everything changed at Brentford once more. McLintock was ousted and Steve Perryman took over at the top. How did you adapt to the new situation at the club?

When Steve Perryman took over it was time for me to leave, Steve didn't like me. As I turned up at Griffin Park on the Saturday of Perryman's first game in charge, somebody came over to say the boss wanted to see me. I walked straight up to his office to be told he was dropping me. He then set about finding me a new club.

I remember my brother came over to my apartment on the Sunday night to pass on a message from Perryman; Roger said "Francis, the boss says that you are training with Wimbledon tomorrow morning…" So I turned up at Wimbledon on Monday morning and I was in their squad to play Aston Villa away the next night. Steve Perryman just wanted shot of me and I think it stemmed from a bust up the two of us had during a pre-season friendly with Spurs before the 1983-84 season. He called me something that I'm sure he would hate for me to repeat in this book and we had a pretty nasty exchange of words when I told him what I thought about his comment. When he became boss the writing was on the wall.

You played back in the late 70s and early 80s, a less tolerant era. As a young black player you must have experienced a lot of racist abuse?

You wouldn't believe some of the things I've had to listen to as a black player. There were times that I would have loved to have jumped the barriers and waded into the crowd, but apart from knowing I'd get a right beating and probably never be allowed to play football again, I knew I had to blank it out and get on with scoring to shut them up.

They may have been throwing bananas at me or calling me a black bastard in an environment where they felt comfortable to do so, but I would have loved to have seen them come down to my neighbourhood and done the same. They wouldn't have survived. To be honest, most of the time comments didn't bother me one little bit, but the worst place I ever experienced abuse was just after I'd joined Reading when we had an away game up at Leeds United.

Talking of ugly scenes, do you remember the afternoon when Bees defender Paul Roberts was punched by a Millwall fan who had come on the pitch after you'd scored?

God yeah, Paul really shouldn't have gone up to the Millwall fans and wound them up. He'd come to Brentford from The Den and I think he was voted their Player of the Season just before he moved to Griffin Park, but after seeing his gesture one of their fans jumped over the fence and lamped him one. I'd made the error of blowing a few kisses to the home end too after scoring the winner, so when the final whistle went, all the Brentford players bolted for the tunnel.

You are held in very high regard among Brentford fans, the loud 'Jo, Jo, 'Av A Go!' chants when you came back for the Griffin Park Centenary celebrations showed what supporters still think of you.

The fans were always good to me at Brentford and I'll never forget the reception I got when I came back from my broken leg against York City and scored my goal. To hear them all singing "Joseph is back, Joseph is back", was amazing, I'll always remember that warmth as long as I live.

Then after the final game of the season hundreds of fans flooded on to the pitch and mobbed me, it was another great gesture, but I have to admit I shit myself a bit because my shirt, boots and shin pads all got ripped off me. I did have a laugh about it back in the changing room though.

I also remember a girl standing up against the barrier shouting at me from the Brook Road stand one game. While I was getting ready for a corner, I heard her scream out my name, so I looked up in the direction the voice had come from. She repeated what she'd shouted, "Jo, Jo, will you pleeeeease, have, a go!" Obviously she didn't think I was trying hard enough, but when the corner was driven in it bounced off my head and into the net. As I looked over she was going crazy.

Will you talk us through your list of clubs after you left Brentford?

After The Bees I signed for Ian Branfoot at Reading, then I went to Sheffield United, then Gillingham, Crewe Alexandra, Fulham, then over to Belgium for a bit. After the full time days I had stints at places like Slough, Chertsey and Walton and Hersham. [Laughs] I've been around a bit.

That's a lot of clubs, but also a lot of experience. I understand you're an ambitious football coach now?

I've had a successful few years coaching the youth side at Wealdstone and we had a lot of press coverage recently when we played Liverpool at Anfield in the FA Youth Cup. I've got my UEFA 'B' coaching badge and plan to do the 'A' qualification in the near future. I'd love to get involved in the professional game again in some capacity as I've got a lot of knowledge to pass on to the next generation. [Smiles] 'Brentford's Striker's Coach' has got a good ring to it!

Looking back, how would you describe yourself as a striker?

Dangerous. You didn't want to give Francis Joseph half a chance because he would put it in the back of the net. Yeah, I like to think that I was a decent football player. I had great pace, which was one of my main assets. I could hold the ball up well and bring other players into the attack and I was brave. But more important than any of those qualities was the fact that I was damn fit.

If it wasn't for the fitness I would have been playing Sunday League football all my life. Hopefully my son Zack can follow in his Dad's footsteps, if he's a chip off the old block then I'll be well chuffed.

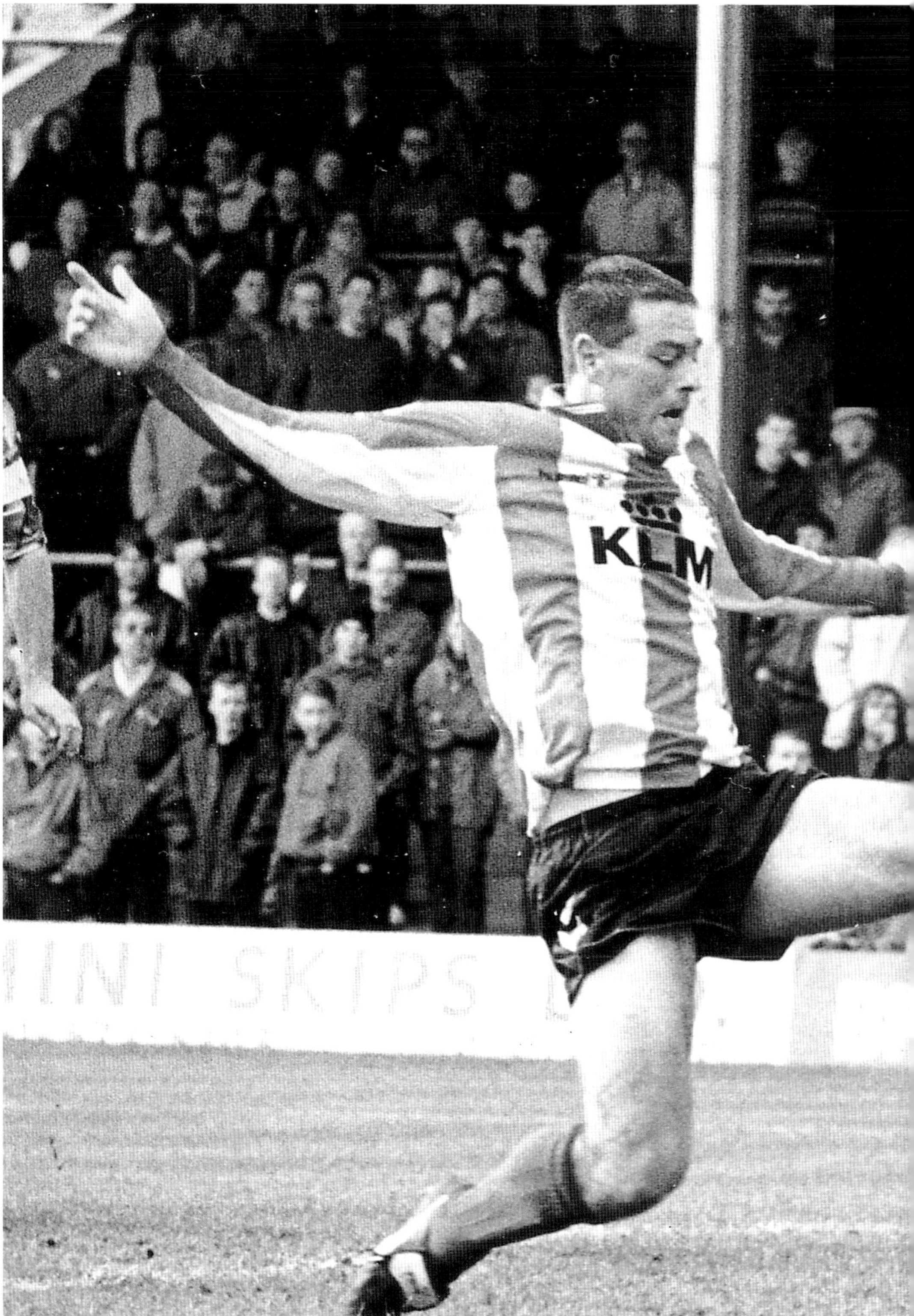
KLM
INI SKIPS

Denny Mundee

Signed by David Webb in his first season as manager, Denny struggled early on, but the utility player's switch from full-back to centre-forward proved very fruitful for the former Bournemouth player. Denny's initial game up front was away at V.S. Rugby in the FA Cup First Round tie in November 1993, and although he didn't score in the torrential three-nil win, Mundee was hacked down for Joe Allon's penalty and demonstrated what a handful he could be for defenders.

In the following weeks Denny started to shine in front of the Bees faithful and showed what he was capable of... It was a case of 'move over Mr. Twaddle, say hello to Mr. Twiddle'.

Mundee's trademark 'Twiddle'- the step-over dummy that seemed to leave defenders scratching their heads every time he tried it - was best used during Brentford's home game with Bristol Rovers in January 1994, everything Denny touched that afternoon was magic. In fact the third goal in his amazing hat-trick is one of the best goals of the past two decades. The way Denny slaughtered the Rovers defenders before curling a beautiful shot into the top corner of the Ealing Road goal was superb.

The arrival of Bob Taylor from Leyton Orient meant Denny was eventually relieved of his goal-getting responsibilities, but the player's 100% commitment remained there for all to see. 'We're not worthy' bowing greeted Mundee's arrival onto the pitch from then on, and whenever he was sub, the New Road choir would sing his name as he limbered up on the touch-line.

Mundee may not have been the greatest player ever to pull on a Bees shirt, but he was one of us, you could tell that Denny would sweat blood for the club and he is assured of a great reception whenever he returns... But as you are about to discover, Denny Mundee joined Brentford in the most unusual of circumstances. Has anyone heard of a welcome quite like this one?

So where did the young Denny Mundee grow up and how did you become a professional footballer?

I grew up in Swindon, although my parents originally came from Shepherd's Bush. I went through all the local divisions as a kid and represented Swindon schoolboys, then a lot of teams came in to offer me trials.

Harry Redknapp was very keen on signing me, I remember he told my Dad that he'd like to offer me a contract for an apprenticeship then two years on professional terms after that. He even said he'd pay a £5,000 signing on fee, which was a fantastic offer and was a fair bit of money back then.

My Dad decided not to tell me about the money as QPR were also in for me. He later said he thought it was best for me to pick the club I felt was right, not be swayed by a cheque and maybe make the wrong decision long-term.

Rangers were in the top flight then and the set up was far better than at Bournemouth, so we agreed I should start at the top, then if things didn't work out, I could always drop down the ladder later on. Harry Redknapp obviously kept an eye on my progress at QPR because after a while he came in for me again and I signed for Bournemouth. I made my debut up at Oldham on the Astroturf, coming on for the last quarter of an hour or so. Then I made my home debut for the last game of the season against Plymouth.

What was Harry like back then, did you learn a lot from him?
I got on well with Harry and over the years I've got on well with all my managers really, but sometimes I didn't agree with how he handled my development. In my first season of regular first team football I was voted Man of the Match by the local press on a fair few occasions, then I'd find myself dropped the next week for an important away game.

Harry had his reasons and perhaps he thought I didn't have the experience to handle some matches at that stage, but it left me confused because I wanted to play in them so I could gain what he thought I was missing.

When did David Webb make his approach to take you to Griffin Park?
It was actually Stuart Morgan, who was running the youth team at Brentford at the time, who suggested to Webb that I was available and could do a good job for him. Stuart had been my manager at Weymouth where Bournemouth had loaned me out in the early days to get me match fit and ready for the first team at Dean Court.

But the transfer to Brentford was a bit bizarre really, David Webb agreed to bring me to the club, but virtually the first thing he said to me was that he didn't really want me; "I don't want any ex-Bournemouth players at my club." I was a bit stunned to be honest, he then sat me down and quizzed me on what I thought of Harry Redknapp. So I told him what I just told you.

Webb then made it quite clear what he thought of my ex-manager, none of which was complimentary at all. There was obviously some bad blood between the two, but Webb certainly had it in for Bournemouth as a club too.

I was stunned really, either he wanted me or he didn't, he was the manager. I didn't know why he'd actually signed me if he didn't really want me and it wasn't exactly the best welcome to a new club.

Then Webb started to pick me as right back in the team because Brian Statham was injured. I was a bit of a utility player at Dean Court, in fact I'd played in every position apart from in goal for The Cherries, but right-back really wasn't my strongest role. Because of that the fans didn't see the best of me in the early days at Brentford.

I think you're right, the fan's jury was certainly out on you early on, but when you were moved up front, that's when your cult status was achieved. Tell us about the position switch.

[Laughs] Well, after Mickey Bennett had that infamous training ground fracas with Joe Allon, Bennett smashing him in the mouth and breaking Joe's jaw, Webby was forced to try me out up front, which thankfully worked out well for me.

The club was in transition during season 1993-94, it was the year after Brentford had been relegated and there was a mix of Phil Holder signed players and Dave Webb's additions. Apart from the unfortunate Bennett-Allon incident, what was the mood like in the camp?
It was good, but talking of Phil Holder, he actually tried to sign me the season before, although the move didn't quite work out. But the mood at Brentford over-all was great, at most football clubs there are little cliques that players are split up into, but I didn't sense that at Griffin Park.

So take us back to the era of 'The Twiddle'. Can you explain how you invented the unique step-over manoeuvre that got the Brentford fans jumping up and down with excitement whenever you got the ball?
[Beaming smile] They were good days, but I can't take the full credit for that little routine, I have to put my hands up and say I copied Glen Roeder. I saw him do it and how easily it allowed him to go past other players.

I used to go out over the fields with my brothers in Swindon and we used to play football for hours, it was over there that I practised the dummy over and over again. I can't really remember the first time I tried it in a league match but I had to be in a confident mood to try it as there were a few times that it didn't work in the early days.

'Denny's Twiddling Master Class' took place during the home match against Bristol Rovers during the 1993-94 season. Brentford eventually lost the match four-three but the fans witnessed a Denny virtuoso hat-trick and a superb all round display by you. Was that the best game of your life?
It probably was. I have to admit I've got that game on video. I don't exactly pop home every lunchtime to watch it, but I do put it on from time to time and I still can't believe that we lost the match to be honest.

I know I got three goals but I should have got a fourth late on to square the match again, my header hit the post. When we pulled the game back to three-all I thought we'd go on and win, but I can still see Kevin Dearden's mis-timed clearance going straight to a Rovers forward who smashed the ball from about thirty yards straight back into the net for their winner.

Season 1994-95 has become infamous among Brentford fans. The reduction of the size of The Premiership that year meant only one team

gained automatic promotion from our division. Brentford were fighting neck and neck for the top spot until the very end but ultimately had to settle for second position and a play-off place. Is it galling to you that in any other year the club would have gone straight up?

Very much so, it was hard to take. But ultimately the games that cost us were the two against Birmingham and losing to Bournemouth at home right at the end which allowed them to pull off an amazing relegation escape at our expense at the top. I think Brentford were easily the best team in the division that season, Birmingham weren't the superior side.

What do you remember of the game up at St. Andrews? With over 3,000 vociferous Bees fans in a crowd of over 25,000, and with only three games to go until the end of the season, it must have been a very nerve-wracking game to play in?

It was the classic six-pointer up at their place and whether the pressure got to one or two of us I don't know. I remember it was very quiet in the dressing room after the game, losing the game was a real set-back.

Brentford therefore had to settle for a two-legged play-off fight with Huddersfield Town, a tie that went all the way to penalties with it's devastating conclusion. The fans struggled to cope with the injustice of Brentford's fate that season, so can you put into words what it was like to stand on the pitch when we lost in that shoot-out?

It still haunts me to this day, especially my penalty miss. Nearly every time I see somebody take a penalty on the television or when the play-offs come round at the end of every season, I get flashbacks. What made it more frustrating for me was that I'd scored a couple of penalties for Brentford against Huddersfield in a league game so to miss the one that mattered most made me feel worse.

I can remember my penalty as clear as anything, I stepped up and kicked the ball to the keeper's left, but for whatever reason there was just no conviction to my shot. I never normally placed them to the right side of goal, I don't know what was going through my head. It wasn't the nerves, if anything maybe I was too confident. That was the third of our penalties, but obviously Jamie Bates had been cast in the unenviable role of missing the last one which sent Huddersfield through to the final at Wembley.

To a certain extent do you think the writing was on the wall for Brentford when we had to settle for the play-off lottery after missing out on the title and automatic promotion?

No, all the players were so confident that we would still go up. The talk in the camp was that we would knock out Huddersfield and that we fancied that Bristol Rovers would turn Crewe over in the other semi leaving us to finish the job off under the twin towers. We really did think we would still go up even though we were disappointed that Birmingham pipped us at the post. We didn't fear anyone in that league, we'd beaten almost all of them during the course of the season and we genuinely didn't see ourselves getting beaten in the play-offs.

It must have been pretty sombre back in the dressing room after those disastrous penalties?
Everyone was so numb, there wasn't a lot said.

What did David Webb do to try and rally the players?
The club paid for all the players to go to Cyprus for a week so we could relax together, have a few drinks and try and get everything out of our systems. But when we arrived in Ayia Napa there was one pretty big problem. On our first night out on the town we discovered that all the Birmingham City players and management were staying in the same town.

We couldn't believe it, Ayia Napa is only a small town and there's only a handful of main clubs you can go to, so every night, there they were, rubbing it in and giving us grief. It was bound to go off at some stage and I was the first to snap, I'd just had enough of the ribbing one night and decided to offer out the main protagonist.

Luckily City's Peter Shearer defused the situation. I guess the easiest thing for us to do was just to avoid them completely but we decided that we couldn't run away and we had to get on with our holiday as best we could. Even with the constant reminder of the lost title race in our faces every night. I remember even the City back room staff were walking around dishing out abuse. I suppose if the tables had been turned, we'd have done exactly the same to them.

Did Webby go out and socialise with you every night?
Not really, we'd have dinner together and that, but after a couple of nights in our cockroach infested hotel, Webb and the management team checked out and moved into something a bit more plush, which was nice for them.

Because of the less than successful summer holiday was there still a dark mood in the camp when you got together for pre-season training?
Those five weeks apart made all the difference I thought, I couldn't wait to get back to the training ground for pre-season training and all the banter that goes with it. Things didn't seem gloomy, a fresh start and all that!

There were certainly signs of a play-off hangover when the new season started wasn't there?
Things didn't seem to be clicking like they had been, you're right. Looking back it seemed like we were getting really punished for our mistakes and we

January 1994: Denny Mundee in action during the 4-3 home defeat to Bristol Rovers

CULT BEES AND LEGENDS VOLUME TWO

January 1994: More action from Denny Mundee's 'best ever match'

Denny Mundee caught mid-twiddle in the rain at Griffin Park

found that instead of being able to win even if we were slightly below par, we'd be losing. Things just didn't seem to gel as they had done.

Your personal situation took a turn for the worse midway through the 1995-96 season too. You had a fairly public contract squabble with David Webb and found yourself forced out of Brentford.

It was a really nerve-wracking and upsetting time for me and my family, yes. I had been offered a new contract and was happy to sign a new deal with David Webb, the sticking point was that I wanted a £5,000 signing on fee so I could afford to buy a new car. I had 130,000 miles on the clock of my old banger and was driving up to Brentford and back every day from Bournemouth.

So Webb told me not to sign the new deal and said that I should go on a week to week contract while he went away and sorted things out for me regarding the fee. Then about two weeks after Paul Davis arrived at the club from Arsenal, Webb called me in to say that the Chairman had told him that the wage bill was getting too high and that I was the easy option to let go.

Webb had insinuated in the local press that you were living some sort of Champagne Charlie lifestyle and you were holding out for more money?

I read what had been printed and wasn't happy. Fact was I was prepared to sign a new deal for Brentford which was exactly the same amount of money as when I'd joined the club, £450 per week. You could hardly live the Champagne life style on that, anyway, I had a wife and three daughters to support. Those reports upset me. That situation left me really disillusioned with football, I knew that some of the other lads were on far more than me and I didn't think that a signing on fee was out of order. I thought the game was bent if I'm honest.

Fortunately you found a new club quickly, signing for Liam Brady at Brighton. The timing of the move meant that you made a quick return to Griffin Park, on Boxing Day 1995. What do you remember about the reception you were given by the Brentford fans?

I can honestly say that the time I spent at Brentford means more to me than any other club I have been at. I spent eight years at AFC Bournemouth but I felt that the Brentford supporters really took to me and it means an awful lot to me to be remembered in a good light.

When I came back to Griffin Park with Brighton after leaving, to hear my name being sung by all the fans in the corner of the New Road stand as I was running out of the tunnel was special. That demonstrated to me that Bees fans were different class. When I'd gone back to Bournemouth I was subjected to some outrageous abuse, one guy even screamed at me that he hoped I'd caught Aids while I'd been living up in London. So to hear my name sung by the Brentford fans and their rapturous applause was fantastic.

How was life at Brighton during that traumatic time for the club?
Brighton were still at The Goldstone Ground when I arrived but it was a weird atmosphere down there. Liam Brady had originally signed me for a month, then because things were working out well, he said he'd get the deal extended. I couldn't believe it when he went and got the sack two days later. Everything was up in the air for me again, so I was very relieved when Jimmy Case took over, as I knew him from Bournemouth.

With all the demonstrations against Seagull's Chairman David Bellotti and the infamous move away from the Goldstone, concentrating on playing football must have been almost impossible on match days?
It was terrible for the players, if we went a goal down at home all the fans would come piling on the pitch and we all had to leg it down the tunnel to safety. The players were petrified, if anyone made a mistake and we conceded it would just go off all round the ground.

We could fully understand the supporters, the players were right behind them. We certainly didn't want to be forced to play our home games at Gillingham either, playing in front of one man and his dog.

Because of injury you were forced to end your playing career at Brighton, can you tell us what happened?
I had started to get a lot of back problems, which meant eventually I couldn't train and could only play with the help of pain killing injections. Then one day the club doctor was walking down a corridor behind me at the club and he noticed the way I was hobbling.

He insisted that I went to the hospital to get an MRI scan straight away. That showed up that two of the disks in my spine had prolapsed and the medical staff wanted to operate on me there and then. The surgeon said it would be a fairly risky procedure which had a sixty percent chance of working.

He also said that if things didn't go right there could also be a chance that I wouldn't walk again. Obviously I couldn't agree to the op there and then so I drove home and talked things through with my wife.

The specialist said that if things went well there would be a chance that I could play again, but my back probably wouldn't hold up to any more rigorous training. I had the op and six weeks later I was back in light training.

But would you believe it, as I was jogging round the pitch soon afterwards, I twisted my ankle and chipped the bone!

I then piled on the weight and ended up looking like Jimmy Five Bellies. The local newspaper down in Brighton ran a story about me being finished, which at the time was news to me, but they ended up being right. I didn't play again.

What did you think when Brentford reached the play-offs at the end of the 2004-05 season?

Brentford cost me a lot of money. I'd put a few quid on The Bees going up, in fact the bookies stung me the previous time too. Perhaps it's me, maybe I'm the jinx, next time Brentford look like going up I'll keep my money in my pocket, that way they'll probably go up as Champions.

You'd left by the time the story broke, but what did you think about the Jamie Bates exposé in the News of the World?

[Laughs] I was gutted to be honest, I'd stayed round Jamie's place quite a few times after nights out, he'd never offered me his wife for £40!

I remember my brother ringing me up and telling me to get down to the newsagents quickly. To be honest I couldn't believe what I was reading, I felt really sorry for Jamie, it must have turned his life upside down and he's a decent bloke at the end of the day.

It was no real surprise to the players when he didn't show up at the Centenary Day at Griffin Park, but it's a real shame that after all those years at the club, and all those games for Brentford, Jamie feels awkward about coming back because of the stick he may get.

What are you doing for a living these days Denny?

I'm a self employed exterior wall coating specialist. I work with my brother who has been doing it for over eighteen years. I used to help him out during the close season when I was playing football, so when I decided to hang the boots up, I got into it full time and learned the trade.

What are your lasting memories of Griffin Park itself?

I think it's a great ground. I always remember looking over at Griffin Park when I was sitting in the back seat of my Dad's car driving down the M4. Although I never dreamed I'd be lucky enough to play there one day. I think it would be shame to leave Griffin Park and get too commercialised, it will be a sad day if the club ever leave.

August 1963: Johnny Brooks scores during Brentford's 4-1 home win against Notts County

Johnny Brooks

Brentford's history over the past sixty year period demonstrates a cyclical 'feast then famine' mentality by those who have controlled our club during that time. When ever a rich knight in shining armour rides into town flashing his jewel encrusted sword promising a new era of growth and investment, a financial crisis is normally just around the corner. These men tend to skip over the fact that they won't actually be using their own wealth to pay for the revolution.

The fanfare arrival of Ron Noades in 1999, then the recession that followed, can be compared to an almost identical situation following Jack Dunnett's spending spree at Griffin Park in the early 1960s, which undoubtedly contributed to the crisis our club faced nearer the end of the decade.

When Dunnett burst onto the scene he promised Brentford fans new hope that he could resurrect the club after slipping from top flight to basement in just eight post-War season. "My directors and I have guaranteed a large sum of money which will bring at least one high quality player to Griffin Park during the close season. When I say high quality I do not mean around £3,000. We mean to buy the best available."

And so it was, for a while at least. Big finances were made available to manager Malcolm McDonald and not one, but two top draw, international standard forwards were brought in to join the mercurial Johnny Brooks who had arrived at the club the previous summer. Several other impressive additions to the squad were also funded.

Brentford fans were treated to some stunning attacking football and it was no surprise that with such an array of talent the side marched straight back out of the division by grabbing promotion in 1963. The new forward line of McAdams, Dick and Brooks had contributed a staggering sixty-nine goals of the team's total season haul of ninety-eight,

Johnny Brooks was a household name in London when he joined Brentford. Having won England caps while at Tottenham he was signed by Chelsea's Championship manager, the great Ted Drake, and played in the top flight at Stamford Bridge. So you can imagine the excitement when he arrived at Griffin Park. For two fantastic years Johnny had Bees fans pinching themselves - they couldn't believe he was one of ours!

Brooks' majestic wing-play unsurprisingly mesmerized countless Fourth Division defenders and with three ex-international forwards terrorising teams up and down the land, the goals rained in every week.

So perhaps it was no wonder that I was told in no uncertain terms by an elderly Brentford fan that "if you do a second volume of your book and don't include Johnny Brooks I will come looking for you!"

Johnny certainly is a true Brentford legend and the provider of some of the most attractive, free-flowing football that Griffin Park has ever had the pleasure of witnessing.

You had a very illustrious career before coming to Griffin Park, playing in the top flight with Tottenham and Chelsea, plus you'd been capped eight times by England. What made you move across West London to join Brentford?

I remember that things weren't working out too well for me at Chelsea at the time, so when Malcolm McDonald came in for me, I decided to give Brentford a shot. I got on well with him too which meant a lot, he was a fair man who knew the game. Because of the maximum wage rules the money wasn't a lot different from what I was on at Stamford Bridge.

How did you find Brentford after being at two of the biggest clubs in London?

Tommy Cavanagh, the trainer who became Brentford manager later on, was a cracking bloke who made us laugh. Tommy would know how to give you a little dig from time to time to get the best out of the players but he knew what to say and when to say it. [Laughs] I remember I used to drive up from Reading every day for training in my sky blue Ford Consul.

Malcolm was good for a player like me, he knew what my game was all about and told me to just go out and enjoy myself. Football wasn't so tactical back then and players tended to stick to their positions in a standard 2-3-5 formation.

It was a bit of a struggle that first season if I remember, Brentford had a very small squad and some of the players just weren't up to it. We got relegated to the Fourth Division at the end that season which was a blow, but it seemed a nice, close-knit club.

Speaking to some of the older Brentford fans they say that the players around you when you joined simply weren't good enough to cope with your skills. Was that the case?

Well I wouldn't be harsh enough to say that, but the side that I played with in the first season weren't as good as the following year. The club brought in some very good players in the summer, then after an average start to the new season, more money was made available to spend on experienced players.

As you say, there were some really big name, big money signings made around that time. Can you talk us through some of them?

My ex-Chelsea team mate, Mike Block, was the first one to arrive, he was a good winger and a fine crosser of the ball. Mickey had come through the youth system at Stamford Bridge and was part of a cracking junior team that had included Ron Harris.

Then over the summer Matt Crow arrived from Norwich City, he brought a lot of experience with him. Although Matty was getting on a bit he had a wise head on his shoulders and helped iron out some of our previous defensive weaknesses. Then came the first of two really big name transfers. Billy McAdams was an Irish International and arrived from Leeds United, then a little bit after the season started, John Dick, who had played for Scotland, came over from West Ham. My eyes lit up when those two arrived.

John was a big, gangly bloke, thick set and all left foot. He knew how to score though, and he liked the horses too. John and myself used to spend a lot of time swapping tips with a bloke in the New Inn pub who owned a couple of horses himself. We liked a flutter and it was dangerous when the cards came out on the coach to away games because I lost my week's wages a fair few times on those long journeys north I can tell you.

So Brentford were able to field a trio of International class forwards in the Fourth Division, that must have been unique?
It was very special at that level and the three of us really enjoyed playing together. We scored a lot of goals in the process. I got twenty-two, John got twenty-four, and Bill got twenty-three during the Championship season. But a lot of my goals were penalties though, that was my job.

I don't think I missed one during the Championship season. The three of us all seemed to click straight away which was an important factor in making it such a special season, the team just fell short of scoring a hundred goals that year, which is pretty impressive I think.

The three of you obviously found life in the basement fairly easy, with that combined experience and pedigree was there a temptation to get complacent or talk about how many goals you'd score before each match?
It was never like that, things just happened naturally. There were some big victories that year, lots of four goal wins plus a fair few fives, so we always went out on the pitch knowing there were goals in us.

Do you remember your goals for Brentford?
As I've admitted, a fair few of them were penalties and they are all much of a muchness, but a few still stand out in my memory. I'll never forget my winner at Griffin Park against championship rivals Oldham when I went round two defenders and curled the ball into the corner of the net, or the two I scored during the nine-nil rout against Wrexham. The Oldham goal really stands out though, the match was a real top of the table clash played in the pouring rain and we won two-one.

A lot of Brentford supporters of a certain age hail you as one of the finest players to wear the club's red and white shirt. It must be nice to be remembered so fondly after all this time?

The crowd were always good to me at Brentford, they really seemed to appreciate me being there and it also means a lot that there's a photo of me in the boardroom for being one of the best players the club has had in the past fifty years. I donated my Championship medal to the club a few years ago too.

Stalwarts like Ken Coote, Gerry Cakebread and Tommy Higginson survived the side's shake-up, how did you rate them?
Ken was a super full-back and a fantastic person I thought. He could have played in the top flight for certain. Gerry was a very good goalie and Tommy always gave you everything he had during a match, you could always rely on Higgy to give you 100%. Every side needs a player like Tommy.

The 1962-63 season will not just be remembered for silverware, but also for snow. The winter of '62 was one of the worst on record which meant after Brentford's Boxing Day win against Chester, Bees fixtures were frozen off for more than six weeks. How did the players stay fit?
There was a hell of a lot of snow that winter and it affected football badly. Believe it or not the players used to run up and down the terraces in the Brook Road stand to help us keep fit, but it must have worked.

By the time we started playing matches again we had a fair few games in hand on Oldham at the top. We had a fantastic run over Easter to catch them up, then beat them to the title by three points.

You missed the tail end of the Championship season through injury. After such an impressive year it must have been a disappointment to miss out on the final few games whilst your team mates finished the job off?
That was quite a nasty injury, I tore my groin running for the ball during a match. I was quite quick in those days, and when I saw a gap to zip in to I would attack it. But this time, as I set off, I felt something pop.

The injury was not only very painful but also looked really bad, the whole inside of my leg filled up with blood. It took me more than three months, the whole of the summer, to come back from that. I missed pre-season and was struggling a bit for form when I returned.

You only played a handful of games for The Bees after coming back before moving to Selhurst Park, why did you decide to leave?
I was in and out of the side at the start of the new season and ironically I made my last appearance for Brentford away at Bournemouth and Boscombe in the FA Cup. I've lived in Boscombe for the past eight years now and love it down here. Crystal Palace manager, Dick Graham, came in for me, which I thought would be a good move. But things didn't work out at Selhurst Park

CULT BEES AND LEGENDS VOLUME TWO

August 2005: Johnny enjoying retirement near the sea in Boscombe

170

and I only played about half a dozen matches and they decided to let me go at the end of the season. Lincoln and Aldershot came in around that time, but I didn't fancy going to either of those clubs.

I then got a call from George Curtis, the ex-Arsenal inside-forward, who was manager at Southern League Stevenage at the time, and he invited me up there. George promised to sort me out a house and a job, plus the appearance money was excellent. In the end I spent five super years at the club.

I then had a stint over in Canada with Toronto City, which was great fun. There was only a handful of sides in the league over there and everyone had to play each other six times in a season, but it was an enjoyable experience.

After football I spent over twenty years working as a messenger for an Israeli bank called Bank Hapoalim where I teamed up with my ex-Spurs pal Tommy Harmer. We had a lot of fun taking letters and packages all round the City of London then meeting up for lunch in the bookmakers.

After I retired at the bank another ex-Spurs mate, Mickey Doolan, who was working for Walthamstow Forest Council, got me a job and I had a five-year stint as a park keeper at Ridgeway Park in Chingford.

I used to love playing football with the kids over the park and encouraging them. I remember one day I was watching a group of fourteen-year-olds having a kick-about match and spotted one lad that really stood out. When they had finished, I walked over to him and asked if a club had picked him up as I was interested in recommending him to somebody.

The lad said that he had just been signed by Manchester United and was about to move up north to start his apprenticeship. A few years later I realised the kid was David Beckham.

Talking of David Beckham, you had a lot in common with the current national captain didn't you? Not only did you both play for England but you also both had modelling deals.

[Laughs] He earned a bit more than I did modelling, but you're right, I was used in a Max Factor for Men hair products advert while I was at Brentford. I think I got £30 for the photos and I got to see my face on billboards all over the country for a short time. That was a strange experience!

How do you look back at your time at Brentford?
I have a great deal of respect for Brentford Football Club and I thoroughly enjoyed my time there. I made a lot of friends at Griffin Park. In many ways the two years I spent at Brentford were my happiest in the game.

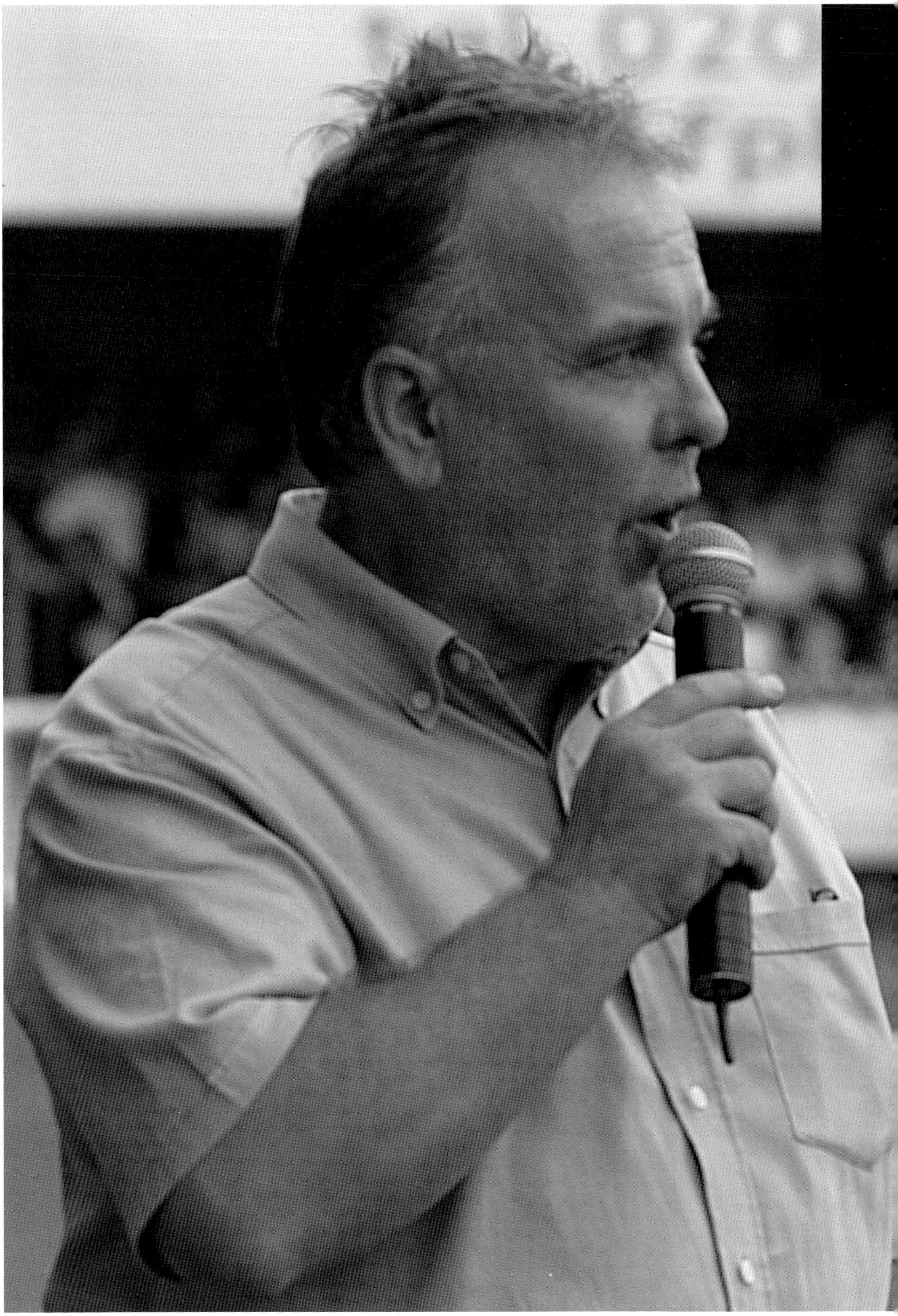

Peter Gilham

I really don't think it's an exaggeration to say that a Brentford match-day at Griffin Park without Peter Gilham is almost as unimaginable as The Bees running out on to the pitch in blue and white hooped shirts. Over the years Peter has become entwined into the very fabric of our football club, and if in the unlikely case you don't know the man by sight, you'll certainly recognise those dulcet tones following numerous years behind the Griffin Park microphone, Clubcall, Sportsman's Dinners or on the odd occasion when you have to ring up the club and buy a ticket for a big match and all the staff muck in. Quite simply, to many people, Peter Gilham is 'Mr. Brentford'.

Loyalty and dedication to the cause is almost impossible to measure, Brentford Football Club means so much to so many fans in so many different ways – but if there was such a thing as a 'Bees Loyalty Gauge', Peter would no doubt measure nine-point-seven on the Brentford Supporter Richter Scale. There really is only one Peter Gilham.

So where did your Brentford roller coaster ride begin Peter?
It started when I was seven, way back in the 1954-55 season. My father brought me along to Griffin Park with my brother Ron for the first time. I've got a really sketchy memory of that era, but I remember Tom Wilson, with his bald head and long shorts. That was the season following Brentford being relegated from the Second Division. We only lived up the road in Ealing, so it was a half-hour walk from our house to the ground, but going to Brentford didn't become week in week out until a lot later.

Towards the end of the 1950s my brother started to play for the Brentford A team, who were in the Seanglian League, with players like Peter Gelson. I used to go and watch his team home and away for a while.

It wasn't until the early 1960s that I started to attend all the home games but I was too young to travel away at that stage because the journeys north entailed an overnight coach journey. By the time it got to the mid-to-late-sixties I would meet up with other fans in what used to be called The Bees Club in Braemar Road at about 11:30pm on a Friday night for trips up to Workington and the like. Then we'd travel through the night, arriving at around 7:30am the following morning.

We'd find a café to have breakfast, have a kick around in a car park, walk around and have a look at the town's market, before going to the game. Then we had to travel back through Saturday evening and half the night to get home, so it really could take up a whole weekend to go to an away match in those days. Saying that the motorway system wasn't very good is an understatement.

I also remember travelling up to Hartlepool on Christmas Day 1966 on the player's coach for their game on Boxing Day. I wanted to go to the match but there was no way of getting there, so I wrote to the manager, Billy Gray, and he invited me to travel up with the team.

Obviously supporting Brentford had become a big part of your life, but when did you actually cross that line and become more involved with the club behind the scenes?

My first active involvement was after the 1967 crisis when a good friend of mine called George Goodser, who was doing the Big Bee Radio match-day music at the time, launched the 'I Back The Brentford' campaign to try and raise funds. It was the Bees United of the day I suppose.

I also started to help a dancing troupe called Alfresco Deo Valante; sixteen girls who did a routine on the pitch marching up and down to De Souza's marching music prior to kick off. I jumped at the chance to get involved there, in fact that's where I met my wife Adrienne, who I married in 1970.

Sue Paine was also part of that troupe, she was the person who organised the famous 1967 Brighton to Brentford walk. Then when George decided to step down from his radio duties at the end of 1968, I got more involved in that area, something I've been doing ever since.

When Frank Blunstone arrived in 1969-70 I sat on the Junior Bees Fun Committee which was set up to raise money to develop the area behind the old Brook Road stand. We wanted to put down a decent surface and erect goals for the junior team to help their training. Eric White was involved with that too, and from then on, I became involved in every testimonial committee with him as well as a few other loyal fans.

I had started to travel to all the away games by that stage, and apart from the couple of seasons after getting married, I've hardly missed a match since. Then when the new Supporters' Association was set up I became the Chairman.

What was the background to setting up the Supporter's Association?

Well the Supporters' Club had been up and running for a number of years but we thought it needed a change of name and to be brought up to date. I was keen to make the club more proactive and give it new impetus. We organised lots of quizzes, film nights and discos and tried to keep the non-match-day social scene as busy as we could.

How do you remember the 1967 crisis? Did you ever think that QPR would pull off their take-over of Brentford which meant our club would be no more?

Well I found out about it like everyone else, in the newspaper. It was like a bolt from the blue for all the fans, we had no idea that the club was in such a terrible financial situation, so the 'paper did us a huge favour in highlighting our position. If they hadn't blown the lid off the story then things may have got even worse and it may have become impossible to save Brentford.

I'm very much an optimist when it comes to bad news and even then I thought there would be a way out of the mire, as I do today with the club's current financial struggle. I always think that if there are enough people who feel strongly enough to save something, then they normally win through. I thought that then and I still think it now.

Do you think you supported a bigger club then than you do today?
Even now, after all those years supporting Brentford, I'm still not sure how big I think Brentford are. The way I see Brentford is personal to me. Although it doesn't compete with Manchester United on the playing pitch, my belief is that Brentford are the only club, the best club. I just know what Brentford means in my heart and couldn't honestly say if Brentford were bigger then or smaller today. Brentford Football Club is the be-all and end-all to me.

So does it matter to you that after fifty years of support, you have only seen your club spend one season outside the bottom two divisions?
It doesn't to be honest. I've said in the past, although I'm not sure I really mean it, that I don't want to see Brentford play in the Premiership. But what I know for certain is that I never want Brentford to lose what makes it so special to so many people. For all that it lacks, Brentford possesses something very precious.

When we get drawn to visit a top flight club it saddens me that the supporters and the players are completely divorced from each other. You watch the game from such a long way away from the pitch that you'd be better off watching it on the television. At Brentford there's genuine camaraderie and I am frightened we'd lose the intimacy if we played in the top flight.

But you must have suffered the same sense of anti-climax and frustration as the rest of the die-hards on countless occasions over the years?
I get over disappointment far better than most people I think. If we lose on a Saturday I just accept that we've lost, but there are people that are very close to me at Brentford whose weekend is completely ruined if the team are beaten. My stance is that you can either put it straight behind you then get on with enjoying the rest of the weekend, or let it eat you up and ruin the whole forty-eight hours. I don't think it's a case of being a battle-hardened Bee or having got used to defeats after all these years, it's a case of us all being different people and that's the way I like to react.

Being such a long-serving and experienced Brentford fan, have you found it hard to bite your tongue in certain situations in recent years when wearing your official Brentford Football Club hat?
It can be difficult yes. I've worked full time at Griffin Park since 1995 and have therefore worked under David Webb and Ron Noades and it was difficult during those times. I had working respect for both men, and like to think it

was reciprocated, but I was in a situation where I couldn't allow my personal thoughts and opinions to interfere with what was happening professionally.

So there have been a few very difficult times, especially the occasion when there was a demo down in the Braemar Road forecourt. That particular day the crowd was chanting for the Chairman to quit, but because he had disappeared after twenty-five minutes of the home game when the side went one-nil down, the crowd then called for the manager. He didn't come out, so then people started calling 'Gilham Out!' I decided to brave it and walk out in front of everyone, but that was hurtful. Over the years I have had to become very careful who I share my thoughts with and who to trust.

I'm sure people like Eric White, the Brentford Press Officer before yourself, didn't have to deal with situations like that?

It's a completely different world communications-wise to the one Eric worked in. In those days irate fans had to write in to the club. They'd go straight to the pub after a game, share their gripes with their friends, then if they still felt strongly enough to post their views in on the Monday morning, they would. They'd get a reply about a week later if they were lucky. Now, with the internet and e-mail, it really is twenty-four-seven. People can write in at any time, day or night, from anywhere in the world, and they expect answers straight away. The internet has made things easier in many respects, but far more difficult and unpleasant in other ways. Some of the abuse and personal attacks that certain individuals mount is unacceptable and I feel sorry for some of the club staff who have to cope with it at times.

If somebody had told you ten years ago that Brentford supporters would be running the football club would you have believed them?

No, not at all, I wouldn't have believed it possible because it's not how clubs were run traditionally. Rich families or the chairmen of successful businesses took over football clubs, never co-operatives of supporters.

It takes a lot of experience to run a successful business, and that is my only concern I suppose; have the fans got the right level of experience to run Brentford? It's one thing to watch the game, it's another to run the club.

But then again, over the years we've had Chairmen running the club who probably didn't have as much experience as we thought they had. Years ago supporters just assumed that if the new Chairman had a few bob then they were qualified enough to do the job. These days fans ask far more questions and demand to know the full story, which can only be good for the game.

But Bees United taking over Brentford is a hugely exciting time, in our perilous financial situation something needed to be done and if the supporters were prepared to work tirelessly to try and put things right then we all have to give them our full support.

On the field, what era do you look back to as your most exciting time as a supporter?

I loved the early 1960s, that was my special time, watching players like John Dick, Billy McAdams and George McLeod. My favourite games aren't from that area, but as a period of time, I loved it.

My favourite all time Brentford game was the FA Cup Fifth Round win up at Blackburn in 1988-89, getting to the Quarter Finals rather than playing in the Quarter Final if you know what I mean.

I think I was more emotional that day than at any other time following the club... What an amazing feeling. Winning the title at Peterborough was special too, but if I had the chance to relive one match, it would be the Ewood Park cup-tie.

Another stand-out moment happened around fifteen minutes before the end of the Sheffield Wednesday play-off match at Griffin Park in 2005 when the supporters realised that a great season was coming to a disappointing end. Instead of making for the exits the Brentford fans stood up as one and started singing and demonstrating their pride for the players and the manager. It was a truly magical five or ten minutes and I'd never witnessed anything like that at Griffin Park.

How about your all time favourite Brentford player?

Ian Lawther. He was a real workhorse for Brentford and didn't get the recognition that some other players received. He was exciting to watch and a very graceful player. Ian was a really nice guy off the pitch too, which goes a long way with me.

How about your all time greatest Brentford line-up?

Dave McKellar, Allan Jones, Hermann Hreidarsson, Sam Sodje, Michael Turner, Dick Renwick, Andy Sinton, Jimmy Bloomfield, Johnny Brooks, Steve Phillips, Ian Lawther. Subs: Paul Smith, Terry Hurlock, Peter Gelson, Jim Towers, Andy McCulloch.

Brentford have had a lot of Managers come and go in recent years, did you become close to any of them on a personal level?

I still get on very well with Wally Downes, and I know he received a lot of stick from the fans before he went, but I've always found him a genuine and decent bloke. To be honest I get on exceptionally well with Martin Allen too. I've got the utmost respect for Martin as a football manager and as a person. Like me he is a passionate man and we get on well together.

I'm like a kid though, I still can't believe I get the chance to talk to the manager and players... It was the same at eight, eighteen and fifty-eight and I honestly think I'm the luckiest guy alive sometimes.

Peter Gilham in action at the Millennium Stadium before the play-off final against Stoke

How about other supporters... Who do you meet on a match-day that makes coming to Brentford so special for you?

Firstly my wife Adrienne, I couldn't have done anything involving the club if it hadn't have been for the missus who has always supported me over the years, she goes to most games with me. I'd also like to mention a good friend of mine, Derek Hazel. I've known Derek for over twenty-five years now and I'd class him as a real unsung hero at Brentford for all he does behind the scenes on match-days and helping with the away travel. I think the world of him as a friend. I also have a number of other close friends, all of whom are an integral part of a match-day at Brentford, and to me personally. You're only as good as the people around you and I'm surrounded by some very special people.

You must have been proud of the way the Centenary Day worked out?

It was a fantastic day and I'll never forget the reactions of the players and witnessing how much they were enjoying themselves. One of the players, Paul Bence, was so emotional that he burst into tears.

I'd spoken to Paul earlier in the day and he was very calm and relaxed about the day, at that juncture I got the impression it didn't mean too much to him, but after he'd spoken to a lot of the fans in Stripes bar, he simply became overwhelmed when he realised how well he was remembered and what his career meant to so many Brentford supporters. I believe that almost every player who has played for Brentford is a hero to somebody and it was great for all those players to come back and witness that for themselves.

Paul Bence was an alright player, not a world beater or anything, but all of a sudden he realised that his football career lived on in the hearts and memories of other people and it was more than just a fading memory in his own mind.

Everyone knows that people like Dean Holdsworth are going to get a standing ovation, and rightly so, players like him are fairly fresh in the memory. For some of the older players, or those who haven't been back to Griffin Park for a number of years, well, I know a lot of them felt ten feet tall when they walked out on to the pitch and were introduced to the crowd.

I like to think that a lot of the ex-players realise what a special club Brentford is, maybe all fans say that about their club, but I genuinely believe that Brentford is more special than any other. Unfortunately it's only once in a blue moon that you get the opportunity, or have a reason, to organise something on that scale, although we will be starting to bring smaller groups of players back to Griffin Park more regularly.

How are you going to feel if we ever leave Griffin Park?

I will feel very, very sad. Griffin Park holds so many wonderful memories for me, and in my eyes you can't beat the atmosphere at Griffin Park under the floodlights for a midweek match. I expect there will also be a sense of excitement, we have seen so many other clubs move to a new stadium and their fortunes have been transformed.

But I am well aware of the fact that many of those examples are the only football club in their town. In our case we are surrounded by competition from other Football League clubs. Brentford is always going to fight an uphill battle to convince people to come and watch us rather than our more illustrious neighbours.

But I would be the happiest man alive if we could find a way to stay here. If we can use the various grants we've been given to raise the capacity and then increase the average attendance figures, then maybe the arguments for staying at Griffin Park would become overwhelming. That situation would make me a happy man.

"The famous Graham Taylor went to Rome to see The Pope..."